A Beaker

NEW AND SELECTED POEMS

A Beaker

NEW AND SELECTED POEMS

Caroline Knox

VERSE PRESS

AMHERST, MA

Published by Verse Press

Library of Congress Cataloging-in-Publication Data
Knox, Caroline.
A beaker : new and selected poems / Caroline Knox.
p. cm.
ISBN 0-9703672-7-9 (pbk.)
I. Title.
PS3561.N686 B43 2002
811'.54—DC21

2002001739

Set in Adobe Caslon
Adobe Caslon is either a registered trademark or
a trademark of Adobe Systems Incorporated
in the United States and/or other countries.
Design by Elizabeth Cogswell Knox

Printed in the Canada
9 8 7 6 5 4 3 2 1

First edition

This volume includes poetry from three previous books:
The House Party (The University of Georgia Press), © Caroline
Knox 1984; *To Newfoundland* (The University of Georgia Press),
© Caroline Knox 1989; and *Sleepers Wake* (Timken Publishers),
© Caroline Knox 1994.

www.versepress.org

Acknowledgments

Some poems in *A Beaker* have been published in journals as follows: "Thérèse Levasseur," *Minnesota Review*; "A Life-Mask," *Verse*; "Phoebe," *Paris Review*; "Hear the Words," *Boston Phoenix*; "Usufruct," "Rose Poem," "Sofonisba," and "Canzone," *Fine Madness*; "*En passant par la Lorraine*," *Cream City Review*; "On Tuesday after Work," "Famous Dog," *Shorelines*; "Sonnet to the Portuguese," *Paris Review*; "The True Meaning," "*Dies Irae*," *New American Writing*; "Angels," *Massachusetts Review*; "*Conversations avec Marceau*," "Tonka," "E," *Columbia Poetry Review*; "A Beaker," *Sycamore Review*; "Cyclades," *East Village Poetry Web*.

The author expresses thanks for a Lannan Foundation Master Fellowship in Literature at the Fine Arts Work Center in Provincetown, for an award from The Fund for Poetry, both in 1995, and for a Massachusetts Cultural Council Individual Artist Fellowship for 1996–97, during which many of these poems were written.

Some poems in *Sleepers Wake* have been published in journals as follows: "Names for the Sun," *Western Humanities Review*; "Chicago 1985," "Kilim," "Nashotah," and "Sleepers Wake," *Paris Review*; "The Comet," *Anglican Theological Review*; "A Test," *Harvard Magazine*; "1989," "Famous Bigshots," and "Itasca," *Western Humanities Review*; "To Celeriack Skinner," *Cream City Review*; "Gorbachev Moon," *Anglican Theological Review*; "Knaves," *No Roses Review*; "October Poem," "Wilma" (winner of the Kay Deeter Award), "A Rune" (anthologized in *The Best American Poetry 1994*, ed. A. R. Ammons), *Fine Madness* ; "The Secular Mask," *Anglican Theological Review*; "Reverse Painting," *New Virginia Review*.

The author expresses thanks for a Yale/Mellon Visiting Faculty Fellowship in 1990–91, during which many of these poems were written, with particular gratitude to John Hollander, the host professor.

Some poems in *To Newfoundland* have been published in journals as follows: "The Stone Calendar," "Log of the *Snow Star*," *New Republic*; "Background," "To Newfoundland," "The Heart," *Shenandoah*; "*Pantoum du chat*," *Ploughshares*; "A Song for Saint Cecilia's Day, 1987," *New Virginia Review*; "Lizzie Borden Through Art and Literature," *Massachusetts Review*; "Beach Poem," *The Red Fox Review*; "Exploring Unknown Territory," *Apalachee Quarterly*; "Movement Along the Frieze," *New American Writing* ("Movement Along the Frieze" also appeared in *The Best American Poetry 1988*, ed. John Ashbery).

The author is extremely grateful to the National Endowment for the Arts, a federal agency, and to the Ingram Merrill Foundation, for support while this book was being written.

Some poems in *The House Party* have been published in journals, as follows: "David," *Anglican Theological Review*; "The House Party," *American Scholar*; "About Calder," *Cream City Review*; "The Cavendish Club," "The Fat Baby," "Nancy Drew," "Green Animals," "I Have Met Freddy," "*Sol Invictus*," *Poetry*; "Fresh Horses Should Be Waiting," "A Poem Beginning with a Line by Wyatt," *Woman Poet: The Midwest*. ("*Sol Invictus*" was a winner of the Bess Hokin Prize of *Poetry*.)

A Beaker

NEW POEMS

A Beaker ... 3

Hear the Words ... 5

Usufruct ... 7

Rose Poem ... 8

En passant par la Lorraine ... 9

Famous Dog ... 10

Sonnet to the Portuguese ... 11

Cyclades ... 12

Thérèse Levasseur ... 13

A Life-Mask ... 17

Our Brains ... 18

The True Meaning ... 19

Tonka ... 21

Gift ... 23

Sofonisba Anguissola ... 24

Angels ... 27

Canzone: Lenses ... 28

On Tuesday After Work ... 30

Conversations avec Marceau ... 31

Phoebe ... 32

E ... 33

Dies Irae ... 34

High Air ... 35

Sleepers Wake
1994

NAMES FOR THE SUN ... 39

CHICAGO 1985 ... 40

SLEEPERS WAKE ... 42

THE COMET ... 44

A TEST ... 45

1989 ... 46

A COOKIE ... 47

KILIM ... 48

NASHOTAH ... 49

TO CELERIACK SKINNER ... 50

THE DEER ... 51

GORBACHEV MOON ... 52

ITASCA ... 53

FAMOUS BIGSHOTS ... 54

KNAVES ... 55

OCTOBER POEM ... 56

THE SECULAR MASK ... 57

WILMA ... 58

A RUNE ... 68

COFFEE TABLE BOOK ... 69

REVERSE PAINTING ... 70

To Newfoundland
1989

The Stone Calendar ... 73

Beach Poem ... 74

Background ... 75

Pantoum du Chat ... 76

Give Me an A ... 77

Railroads and Newspapers ... 78

A Song for Saint Cecilia's Day 1987 ... 80

Lizzie Borden Through Art and Literature ... 84

Exploring Unknown Territory ... 85

Log of the *Snow Star* ... 90

The Heart ... 91

To Newfoundland ... 92

Movement Along the Frieze ... 97

The House Party
1984

I Have Met Freddy ... 101

The Fat Baby ... 103

Nancy Drew ... 104

A Poem Beginning with a Line by Wyatt ... 105

The Prudence Crandall House in
Canterbury, Connecticut ... 106

Fresh Horses Should Be Waiting ... 108

David ... 109

The Cavendish Club ... 110

Green Animals ... 113

Rachel and Wally ... 115

The House Party ... 116

Sol Invictus ... 119

About Calder ... 121

A Beaker

NEW POEMS

A Beaker

The rim flared, but only just:
set it down as it is, small as it is,
three and a quarter inches high,
a silver cup banded with a gold wash.
Beaded at either edge; two italic inscriptions.

The first, a shield of arms:
three crescents with stars between their horns,
a star above engraved upon the body.

Memento John Saffin Junior
  Obijt 9 Dec 1678

Memento: the unlooked-for and predictable;
Obijt: the death of Saffin's namesake child;
9 Dec: early, unlooked-for winter;
1678: Boston, a city upon a hill.

Philosophy abides here in cones of light,
Old Light, in consolation
sermons that smell of the lamp.
His wife Martha lingers but then follows the son—
"I am so sick of this pleasing vanitie"
—a curious gilt knot, wedlock and the death of children.

ooooo

In due course
comes now Hugh Hall,
son of the Governor of the Barbados
and a 1713 graduate of Harvard College;
Hugh Hall buys the late John Saffin's cup
at auction in 1710 from his effects.

Now heavy-jowelled,
as Copley drew him (1758),
a grandfather standing godfather,
in a rose-breasted grosbeak vest and a suit of green,
he causes a second inscription to be made
in a language understanded of the people, thank you very much:

The Gift of H. Hall Esqr. to Hugh Hall Clark
(as in the Catechism: Question:
What did your godparents then for you at this time?
Answer: Silver cup, plate, and spoon.).

The coat of arms above the second inscription
in almost cursive italics,
a patently oval wreath system
of stamped laurel and grain awns,
with a crescent above and a shield
bearing a tiny, articulated Lamb of God
making its way through the mindset of Addison and Steele:
the deist heavens declare the glory of God;
the sensible firmament showeth his handiwork.

Hear the Words

Hear the words of David Shapiro
in *The American Poetry Review*
on the lines of Barbara Guest:

"She uses her Stevens-like tercets
to give pressure and principle
to the topic of restlessness."

Shapiro quits these lines forever
now, an opportunity for travel.
Here's how the rhyme scheme goes:

abcdefghijklm
nopqrstuvwxyz&.
Chris Gilbert put it this way:

"We are two griots at an intersection."
Chris won the Whitman back in '83
and has been a therapist in Worcester, Massachusetts,

right near Grafton, stomping ground of Frank O'Hara.
But "Oh," wrote the latter, "how I hate/
subject matter." How's that for pressure and principle?

Or this: "I read O'Hara to keep myself honest,"
said Kenneth Koch, as in Bob Marley's phrase
"upful and right" (an improvement on the Psalmist),

and Bob's your U.K. uncle. Good on him,
and good on the sculptor Peter Rockwell,
who was two years ahead of me at Putney School,

and who said, "I have never seen a better definition
of open space and enclosed space
than the snow falling indoors through the dome of the Pantheon."

Usufruct

The new ordinary is a Cauliflower.
Freddy has had his girandoles electrified.

"We listen to the sleeping world,"
as *Requiem Fauré Nun*, by Gabriel Fauré.
The closet is full of cossacks.

My mother has a usufruct, actually.
Her high-tops are in the brisker.
We live in that smaragdine pile up there on the hill.
No, we don't—we live in a teensy apartment.

Rose Poem

If indeed "New York is a rose in the heart,"
as a speaker invented by the beautiful and distinguished
Edna O'Brien has it, what is California?
It is a state of grace where, by the sheer Pacific, rosebushes
   inhibit erosion

as citrus scurvy. Now the sun, your star that rose this morning,
promotes photosynthesis through the serrate leaflets' stomata
beneath, which we have known since high school biology.
So the outsider longs for the flower

in happiness and good temper: Rosa Bonheur.
Be modern, rose, be modern with Modern Art;
a game! a dream! don't die on me, don't die on us
in overdocumented youth; give the I-narrator your dominant
   impression, oh platitude.

And oh, Pete Rose, some envoy for baseball, if you read this,
   and I hope you will,
but even if you don't, it is a figurative rose pogonia,
which it turns out is a member of the orchid family native to
   North America
and not a rose at all. This is the posy of a ring.

En passant par la Lorraine

trying to make Aix by suppertime
not really a pilgrimage but a larkishness

avec mes sabots dondaines
I'm the oblate of these wooden
reliquaries and they're killing me

rencontré trois capitaines
over macaroni is a nice mundane inn

Ils m'ont appelée vilaine
Their epaulettes   I spit upon them   the scrambled eggs
avec mes sabots dondaines   *oh oh oh*

Je ne suis pas si vilaine
a monkey wrench in your quiches, messieurs
Evidently you do not
comprehend the signification
Maybe you take me for the
herbaceous boarder *parmi les parterres*
C'est la dernière fois que je vous fais la classe
car le prince de Lorraine
back from seven years in Spain
m'a donné pour mes étrennes
un bouquet de marjolaine
Maybe *that's* where they got the herbaceous boarder idea

Famous Dog

The snow light lights the inside
of the dark house from outside
and the outside snow is a muff
banking the fieldstone facing.
My dog's glinty husky eyes hang
in the deep shade of his fur. We are outside.

Inside the shade of the deep house
little cousins wrapped with their books in quilts
sleep by the coldest light of all,
the television, a polar star.

The husky dog is a candle of the winter light
and heat in the winter massed dark.
My hand sinks in his deep ruff;
we trot like this, interdependent,
over the snow crust;
we trip and drop deeply.

I see the snow weight and weigh the long
conifers, but the husky dips his ruff
and sees just the snow track.

Famous dog, let's go back.
Famous dog, I'll give you a
marrowbone, energy for your dreams.

This light will hold all month.
This month will end the year.
A skylight will open.

Sonnet to the Portuguese

No charts nor maps were accorded
him, so he fabricated a route,
a Maginot Line around the earth.

North he went to Schloss Dreyer-Lindt,
schussing and singing down the isobars,
mit mittened nymphs (aw the pwecious dollins):

"He weareth the graph paper by way of shirt;
he doeth his geometry homework upon the tattersall."
They toasted their *après-ski* tootsies on the Sensenbrenner.

South he went to Las Percales,
which is admired for its clement atmosphere
with Bruce Springsteen and Somerset Maugham,
Gardner McFall and Shelley Winters.

"I'll have a double Branch Rickey, please, with a twist!"
The artisans gathered around him as he spoke.
What was he supposed to do—sit on his hands?

> "Dear Portuguese people, who live in the suburbs
> of Lisbon, painting birds on useful jars
> ultimately sold beside the curbs
> of—gardyloo!—the refuse and the cars
> which take no note in haste to the ballet;
> dear civilization that gave us Zurbarán
> and a Yankee diaspora thick with snapper blues
> in the latitude of the Celestial Snooze:
> when Adam delved," he with the feat of Klee
> continued, "who was then the gentleman?
> Oh, blessed are they in Portugal who sneeze!
> It's Birthington's Washday, and time to tap the trees."

Cyclades

SHE: We are pedaling along the Aegean
        Ocean, over and among the Cyclades.

HE: I am cycling over the Cyclades
        with my beloved, in her pedal pushers.

SHE: That is to say, my pedal pushers
        are on me. My love, for his part,

        wears his jeans in the Cyclades.
        Two pindots represent his eyes.

HE: I push the pedals, Snead of the Slopes!
        Our picnic is devoid of cyclamates.

SHE: We look into the Aegean deep.
        We see the Bony Eel of Moray.

HE: Our picnic is retsina and cheese (*fait accompli*)
        interesting hard bread, olives, sausage, fruit.

SHE: Our picnic is *salade niçoise*
        as on p. 157 of *The Sun Also Rises*.

HE: (Two lines in ancient Greek.)
        (Two lines in modern Greek.)
        Two pindots represent her eyes
        in the old Cycladic guise.

Thérèse Levasseur

This waitress, this laundress
from the Hôtel San Quentin,
this Thérèse Levasseur is,
says the philosopher,
"someone with whom I can
identify myself: an auxiliary of my own flesh."

She is twenty-two, pretty, and a figure of scorn
to all at the hotel—unlettered, untaught,
a waitress, a laundress.

"When I first saw her shyness and sweetness,"
confesses Jean-Jacques Rousseau,
"I told her I never would abandon her.
I told her I would never marry her.
She bestowed on me a tenderness,
and Pleasure became Happiness."

Now Thérèse is no longer a sweetheart,
but a resident mistress, a settled
companion. In all but name, a wife.

"Our affection," writes Rousseau,
"grew with intimacy,
and every day we felt more keenly
we had been made for one another:
our walks in the country, our tavern
suppers, the window-seat meals;
at home, bread, cheese, fruit, wine,
chestnuts, salad, coffee.
We have a spinet, a canary
in a cage, beds covered with
striped cotton. A blanket chest and chairs."

"I tell you, she has a store of common sense
and keeps me and leads me
and protects me from my dangerous
and passionate compulsiveness.
She has the heart of an angel,"
says Rousseau, doing up her corset stays.

　　This is a French poem, so it has a refrain.
　　"He put our five children in the Foundling Home.
　　He gave the money for the education.
　　The midwife took them to the orphanage."

"Please borrow my Plutarch, dear Countess, but do not lend it.
Please send a dress for Mlle. Levasseur."

In Switzerland, a dignified and symmetrical
house, with good-sized gardens, The Hermitage;
fields and orchards, walks, the forest.

"She is happier than she has ever been.
The day we were united was the day
I chose my moral being. But I have never felt,"
says the Citizen of Geneva,
"the least glimmer of love for Thérèse Levasseur.
When I die, all my property belongs to her."

"What excellent coffee I drink at the chateau
with my Thérèse in the peristyle,
my cat Minette and my dog Sultan in company.
Oh, lovely dog Sultan, sensitive, disinterested, and good-natured."

　　This is a French poem, so it has a refrain.
　　"He sent our five children to the Foundling Home.
　　He gave the money for the education.
　　The midwife took them to the orphanage."

"A little, lively, neat French girl," opines James
Boswell of the forty-three-year-old
Thérèse. "A heart like mine," opines
Rousseau, as he and Boswell dine on succulent
vegetables, gigot of lamb, with thyme,
fresh trout from the river Arneuse,
quail, woodcock, the flinty white
wine and the Spanish red.

"My heart," Rousseau declares, "has always
been hers, and this will not change.
We will share our sorrows,
and if Mlle. were not here, M. Boswell,
I would tell you my opinions of women."

James Boswell in bidding farewell:
"I shall never forget your accomplishments.
You weave. You cook. You sit at the table.
You make jokes. You get up; you clear
the table; the dishes are washed; all is
tidy and Mlle. Levasseur is with us again."

As Boswell disappears, she says,
"M. Boswell, shall you see M. de Voltaire?"

ooooo

The voice of Jean-Jacques is aging and infirm:
"We carry rabbits in the rowboat to the little island
to renew the vanishing wildlife. Here at Môtiers,
I make silk ribbons on a little machine
with the women, my new entertainment,
and with Minette my cat and Sultan my dear old dog.
I reside with my nurse Thérèse, of honest and upright heart.
These ribbons I bestow on the country brides,
who must promise me to breast-feed their children.
Man is born free, but everywhere he is in chains."

This is a French poem, so it has a refrain:
"He took our five children to the Foundling Home.
He gave the money for the education.
The midwife took them to the orphanage."

A Life-Mask

Up from just such glop as this
our antecedents oozed into their lives,
glop of the world to make a globe a head,
in a deft pudding production.

This glop is alginate, like bisque, what?
—seaweed on the epidermis, epidermis of the geode.
"Edeog eht fo simredipe, simredipe eht no deewaes,"
I managed to get out.

      OK, pieface:
some of the shaded sectors are gray areas,
arroyos, sierras, or aretes.
And Publius Ovidius Schnozzo, he is the main feature.

Our Brains

Our brains are made of marbles, and a game
is always going on inside our skulls.
A raddled stress like that in billiards pulls
them forward in carom and orbit, over and home,
as changes ring and canons bank and pass
back to the starting place from which they come.
Science Times on Tuesday addresses these same
marbles. A Fourier Transform Infrared
Spectroscope will tell you how old they be,
as old as Agatha Christie; or how dead.
Marbles aren't marble anyway—they're glass,
a liquid indolent and refractory
      as sleet or amortized hail in the cadence of years.
      But a diamond will scratch your idea on the crystal spheres.

The True Meaning

Oh, photographing settlement patterns from the air
as in a balloon—as soon as you have characterized them,
there is a trend away from them in the business world—
and rather than go on to the next
figure to yourself to settle yourself
in this recent fixture, a midden and a walled place
with little streets or traces of streets you can make out going down
    and aim for.

The visionary is there to extend greetings,
Frobisher by name, who has done a lot of articles.
Shyly he approaches by the statues of imported lava.
He writes in a wildcat quarterly
and has made quite a name for himself although sort of a
    tabloid one.

Who would ever make statues of imported lava?
"Fourteen is considered a valuable number here,"
says Frobisher. He encases culture in little vignettes:
"Just a minute, Mrs. Pappadakis, we have a lady here
    who speaks Greek,
Jenny, and we'll put her on the line
so you can explain to her what the matter is."
And the fourteen philosophers are encased, too, what a
    bunch of farmers,
the Lord be thy something-or-other
symbolic and profound. I wish I had recorded
some of the things they said, but you can't always do that.

Yet I recall the hours with Frobisher.
He told me the true meaning of superficial.
There is no plot, only subplots (fourteen of them),
each more apparently inane than the last,

we are content to know from apprehension
of the traditional songs which form their onlies.
But Frobisher sinks in civil esteem.
He mentions something like throwup
when people are already talking about concertos.

You *have* to be polite, and you *can't* be unfair to people.
I'm tough, I can rough it, I'm the best fake you ever met.
For the people there don't need it, can't have it, don't
    like it anyway—
I want to be at home with the people I associate with,
not like lots who go on adventures.

Tonka

On the broad broadloom,
a child impels a large Tonka;
it's a brownish truck,
a UPS Tonka. "How's
Mac?" "Good," he says. (He *is* Mac.)

MacArthur said, "I
shall return." Harry Truman
said, "You bet you shall."
When Harry delivered this,
his tool was rage, not the tank.

(Bess said, "I *won't* tell
him to say 'fertilizer';
it's taken me all
of these twenty-five years, sir,
to get him to say 'manure.'")

So MacArthur retraced
the track back to the redoubt,
who had once been heard
to say elsewhere, "Lafayette,
we are here," in another

context, and that chief
was not the Cincinnatus
de nos jours. His con-
stituents said, "Give 'em hell,
Harry," and so Harry did,

if you'd please excuse
his French. It was Eisenhower,
it was Ike, as I
recall, who put "under God" in
the Pledge of Allegiance, though.

I like Ike OK.
He said that the DAR
could not inhibit
Marian Anderson's song
in their frosty bailiwick.

Yours truly and intrusive-
ly avers that all this stuff is over the head
of the young Mac met
back in stanza 1, but yet

time may provide that
with diligence said Mac may
select role models
for art and/or commerce high
as any Motown icon.

Gift

The snowy globe rotates
in true and short imagist fashion
obviating prosy and secular freight.

As we speak, the flakes, keeping to cold orbits,
are grounded ultimately on a
terra firma base
made in China
made of plastic.

Sofonisba Anguissola

She says to herself,
if you can write A, B, C, you can
presently write S, O, F, O, N,
I, S, B, A. If you can write your
name, you can paint its serifs to sign
Sophonisba (the Carthaginian spelling).
Five Renaissance sisters, and little Asdrubale,
from the quality of Cremona, source
of silk, velvet, fustian; with the need for five dowries:
"excitement and inconvenience." She says to herself,
if you can write your name, you can paint a
witty, inscrutable monogram:
E, R, A, C, K, Y, M.
—has a male soul been born
here in a lady's paintbrush?

You can write AMILCARE, your father's name,
she says to herself. Not the Roman princes' line,
but classical Carthage: transalpine Hannibal,
Hamilcar, Hasdrubal, Sophonisba—
glorious, brave, and ancient losers to Rome.

"If you can draw a laughing girl"
(writes Michelangelo in Rome to Sofonisba in Cremona),
"you can draw a crying boy. Draw one."
Sofonisba is twenty-two; her mentor is seventy-nine.
"Most magnificent and honorable Michelangelo"
(so runs Amilcare's letter), "I am more grateful
to you for introducing her to painting
than for wealth or splendor. May we prevail
on you to send a sketch to Sofonisba
which she may reproduce for you in oils,
oh great and talented beyond all men?"

She says to herself, "If you can draw a laughing girl"
(teaching an old woman to read),
"you can draw a crying boy"
(bitten by a crab from a basket of same,
accompanied by an almost-smiling, concerned
sister). The others say, "She has contributed to the genre
of genre painting." "She has invented" (they say)
"an invention." They say, "*Ars sine scientia nihil est.*"

Sofonisba's drawing is complete.
Boy Bitten by a Crab, Baby Asdrubale:
pain and surprise in the three-year-old's face
and sister isn't entirely sympathetic,
the gazer notes; this is comedy of manners—
sister has mixed feelings.

ooooo

"Will you not consent to this?"
(so runs the letter from Madrid),
"to send your favored daughter Sofonisba
as tutor in painting to the Queen,
she who was Isabel of Valois, young
consort to Philip? Will you send her to Spain?"

Amilcare will send her to Madrid.
"A refusal will be difficult to justify."
In 1560, across the Alps
in a sedan chair, in an Armada ship:
two ladies, six servants, and two gentleman cousins.

"On the night of the royal wedding"
(so writes the envoy of the duke of Mantua),
"the king proposes a dance, the galliard.
No one seems to offer to begin.
So signior Ferrante Gonzaga asks
the Cremonese lady who paints and stays with the Queen.
They lead the dance and open the way for others."

A courtier whispers to another courtier,
"Take a more decisive position against the Huguenots."

The Queen is fourteen. She begins to draw at once.
The king is young, serene, and blond.
Sofonisba draws Isabel, the king, half-length, full.
She paints for the Pope and sends her work to him.
"I wish the brush could represent
the beauty of the Queen's soul to your eyes,
Your Holiness. Insofar as I can tell it,
I have shown you the truth of the Queen."

Soon the Infantas, Clara Eugenia
and Catalina Micaela, are born. And their
mother dies of influenza. "Sofonisba
does not want to go on living." The
gloves of mourning have gussets on the fingers
to display the many mourning rings of jet.

ooooo

From the notebook of Anthony Van Dyck,
on pilgrimage to Sofonisba in Palermo
(it is 1624; she is ninety-two):
"She tells me, 'Do not paint too close,
too high, too low; this way the shadows
of the wrinkles will not show too much.'
She places her nose very close to the painting.
Her hand is steady, without any trembling."

Angels

Angels are God's secretary and sing or multiply and impart
    intelligence.
This of the current instant commends me to you justly and you in
    Dusenberg to Personland.
It says Salzburg on your pajamas. Fall, dream a dream, you're
    C. S. Lewis.
Beloved pets are analogues. Angels
strafe Calvin like jealots as he in the sixteenth century
them! They receive no cult, nor oughtn't. They're not what
    you think.

If secretary, then historian. The alligator is her or his
own pocketbook, the islands are a map of themselves,
and the message pierces our ears; so for Chiliasts, ur-debutantes,
this isn't exactly exhaustive. But it looks up to angels, agents
    of kisses,
in REM sleep and non-REM sleep superseding The Other.

Gross nacre intaglio on angels' fretted shawms!
What Northrop Frye called "the mysterious ephod,"
they don't possess, because they're not supposed to. Ephods
    are for priests.
Still God, the God of their choice, chooses these muffkins
(the angels, I mean) to exteriorize. Consider the pacific
noise and trust stored in only one or two of them.

Canzone: Lenses

I came in the open door, which was the color of the sky,
and walked in half-darkness to what looked like an open
fire, but it wasn't a fire—it was the sky
in a prolific sunset, an apostrophe of sky.
Then I took off my shades, a distorting form of curtain,
and looked out the window beyond at the sky.
But I might as well have been on the Isle of Skye.
I could hardly see as far as the door
without my contact lenses, which I'd lost. The door
was open, but I couldn't see it: a sky
that wasn't even there, a hypothetical window
in my mind. That's what it was like, a window.

Who is responsible for cleaning this window?
I railed grumpily, "lowing at the sky."
In the twilit dusk, it was as if the window
were wearing shades: the Ptolemaic window
of the passé universe, vertiginously open.
Thank God for Copernicus, who was a window
of reason. Ptolemy and his ilk were a window
of received texts. But they were a curtain-
raiser to modern thought, at any rate. The curtain
is up for good now, and the Anderson Window
of high technology has come in the door,
and if you ask me, more power to the door.

It had been raining in through the window and the door.
Lucky for us we had gotten the window-
seat treated with Scotchgard. At length the door-
sill creaked, and my aunt was at the door.
"Oh, eyewash," said that worthy when consulted on the sky
problem. "You couldn't hit the broad side of a barn door.
Where did you have your lenses last?" From the door,

flashes in the sky worked dully in the open
curtains, and I flung the sashes open.
We hadn't seen the Aurora Borealis since up in good old Door
County, Wisconsin (where Jeremiah Curtin
grew up, in part), back in the sixties. A theater curtain,

these northerly phenomena were a theater curtain,
as if there were a gel on the spotlight at the door.
But soft lenses, made of fancy plastic, are a shower curtain
between your retina and reality, fortunately. A curtain
of faith and/or grief, a nimbus around the window
of relative objectivity. But when the curtain
is drawn, there you are, shaking, with nothing to curtain
you, if you lose your lenses. When you find them, the sky
comes back to you through a mirror or a sky-
light. Over these musings, however, let us draw a curtain.

With my eyes wide open, and with (I hope) an open
mind, I drizzle saline solution in my open
and somewhat sanguine eyes, propped open.
Then I sit down and actually begin to read *Curtain,*
a late Agatha Christie, following with *The Open Door,*
by the amazing Ruth Gordon, and then open-
ly and with intensity, *The Picture of Dor-*
ian Grey, by Oscar Wilde, which is open
to page 89: "Dorian Grey listened, open-
eyed and wondering." I open another window.
All this in the spacy time sense of *The Rear Window,*
which my aunt had long ago taken me to the open-
ing of. Or the dizzy space sense in *The Big Sky,*
by A. B. Guthrie, which sees everything in terms of sky.

"Mackerel sky," goes the adage, "mackerel sky,/
Never long wet,/ Never long dry." An eye-open-
er, as well as a cliché, like the Iron Curtain.
Later, of course, I find the damned lenses behind the window-
seat, the one I keep coming back to by the door.

On Tuesday After Work

Lee and Chris and Leslie and Alex (Alexis)
and the people in the next apartment (Page, Tracy, Frankie,
    and Lou)
laden from Super Stop & Shop,
got in Lou's pickup in Grafton
and drove at forty miles per hour max
on 122A and 122,
123 and 118,
on beautiful Rt. 6, on 81,
and so on down to the shore to camp,
content and weary with food and drink and cold.

Wednesday
they woke as one to the monumental whirr
of a great parti-colored globe rising over them as the sun.

Conversations avec Marceau

Oh, Hatshepsut, it is your turn to play
senet with young Horus here and Thoth.
Where are the x? They are in the y.

You hold in your hand the proxy of our view:
        the group is the text
        at the Colorado School of Mimes.
Our friends are such formidable coreligionists
they have a chasuble on the grand piano
and carpeting that doubles as furniture—
you wear showshoes, unless you want to go to sleep.

My "spouse" is of the Druid faith;
when I want his advice, I'll ask for it,
as cassettes about metaphysics snap into your brain
        when you are full of love
                like light into the public library.

Phoebe

Paul the Leader
at Corinth said,
"Phoebe, please go to Ephesus.
You have a new job there.
Tertius, my amanuensis,
please take a letter." This
Tertius wrote down the instructions on the desk in his lap.

"Here, Phoebe, my very competent deaconess,
take this letter to Ephesus."
Paul gave her the letter sealed in red.

So Phoebe ran fast across Macedonia, Thrace, and the Troad,
as if she had
wings on her sandals and cap,
to the beautiful Temple at Ephesus.
There was the Statue of Artemis.
Phoebe saw cows,
limes, lemons, ropes of garlic, figs,
camels, goats, sows,
fowl and fish, pigs.

And Phoebe ran fast right straight
through the Temple and out into the air
and in the gate
and up the stair
to the home of the Church at Ephesus
and gave the Leader the letter.

E

Ruddy, she curtails
the octave intervals,
acclimating
to the parlor upright.
She combs out the snarls
with the letter E.
She plunks the good
theorbo.

> After to have snipped
> the copious sward,
> his hands still ring
> with the Briggs & Stratton.
> He faxes her this sestet
> by the midnight oil.

Dies Irae

An end to vacations in Ostend, an end to memorizing
all of Keats's "Endymion," an end to weeding calendulas.
An end to it: spending at Henri Bendel, an end to fat rear ends
for some people. An end to telephone blunderbores, an end to
stones flying through the air toward injuries. An end
to problems of the endocrine gland, an end to having to
know all endings for cases and tenses, and an end to tension.
An end to irresponsible benders, but no end to a
new blender which blends splendidly. Perpend:
an end probably to the enclitic *ne,* an end to the expensiveness
    of endive.
As a pendant lost from a chain's end, an end to mendaciousness.
Day in, day out, an end to endless wrath, an end to a century,
    and a millennium;
an end to strife anent human rights, an end to endemic hate.
An end to codependence, an end to the word endomorph.
An end to demented emendations, and on to an amendment of life.

High Air

"The scenery is wholly mineral,"
aver the tireless Fosters, the biographers
of Alexandra David-Neel and into the bargain
of the Lama Yongden, her adoptive son;
and, as is said in Tibet,
"This coldness will keep the tea from pouring,"

and never mind about the yak butter.
"The whole world seems strangely far off,"
wrote Alexandra, in residence among
the Reformed Red Hat Nuns of Tibet, "a whirlwind of atoms,"

and among proverbs on the subject of proverbs:
"The peaks are our sentinels," on the roof of the world.
Many Tibetans said this often, as gongs on location.

Ceremonial horns to announce the great
were so long they needed acolytes to support them.
Bells of rare alloys rang, and
bandits abounded there, called Gologs
(which means Heads-on-Backwards).

Now is revealed to Alexandra,
alpenstock in hand, the ascetic
mysteries concealed in a gnostic language:
Of white jade: one ruined effigy in beatified air, high air.
Of green jade: a lotus blossom, and coarse, rubber-like stems;
    a scepter? a weapon? —both.
Of black jade: a torso, a pillar, a jamb figure; no! a cipher.
Jade in substance the meeting of heaven and earth—
"I have seen the world's map and the soul's charts."
Entry ultimately into the city: "Lhasa's prayer is ended.
    Love is now invited."

Sleepers Wake

1994

Names for the Sun

Come all ye brave stargazers on your porches:
the sun today in its own favor
will set with tropical repetitiveness
under cover of dark down in San Antone.
The sun is the third person, the sun has long hair now—
no, short, or if not hack hack.
The sun is a New Critic; it has a Fulbright this year; do tell.

As to particles, it is a picklock. As to rays,
well, there you are—motes and beams.
The sun is a Trafalgar man
and shines in Philly,
where it is a reification
of the epiphenomena.
Joseph Mallord William Turner
(1775–1851)
said, "The sun is God."
Kooky sun-seeker, can you feature it?

Damn it, the sun has a Fulbright every year,
and will set down in San Antone today
in the desert by the significant estuary.
Names for the sun (not that it needs them,
but the game is worth the candle):
beanmonger, set piece, Fellow of the Royal Society.
In its own favor the sun of good report
ends pretty much where it began:
a gift, your lovely and textured gift, because you've been such
    loyal consumers.

Chicago 1985

Here are the parrots, she says, which Mayor Washington,
who lives up there, the Mayor of Chicago,
in that apartment on Lake Michigan
(a sunny seventh floor), here are his parrots
on South Shore Drive. Mayor Harold
Washington, he lives there when he's here
but his parrots live there all the time
in their parrot apartment house
which looks like a bale of hay in a tree
with doors in it with parrots in them.

That's what *she* says, anyway, and he says
his Old and Lousy Railroad Joke. And here
it is, he tells us. Man comes into little
southern railway station. "I've got to
get to Chicago in the worst way." "Take the Nickel Plate."

Yet not to be outdone, this third voice says
his Early Early Sixties Joke to us.
RFK and JFK
and Mayor Daley the First are in a chopper
over Lake Michigan fairly near O'Hare.
The engines conk completely out,
and there's only one parachute.
So they vote on who will get it,
and Mayor Daley the First wins, nine to four.

On a Fairfield Porter Day, she says,
a qualified Yankee writes this trope of flight,
which dedicates itself to Steve
Goodman, who wrote "The City of New Orleans,"

who came from Chicago, the city theme and text
and adversary subject matter, where Hoosiers
range all along the southern border.

Why don't the parrots go south, she says.

Finally, here is something that is true.
In nineteen hundred sixty-seven,
Mayor Daley the First said to Gwendolyn Brooks,
"People think that Picasso hates Chicago,
and that is why he inflicts his pictures on us.
Write a poem for us about Picasso."

Sleepers Wake

Karen made a poem
walking to rehearsal
about children making angels
seeing angels in the chimney flames
Karen is the tall one
with braids down her back
She's old enough to be
like a lady and have the braids
on her head like a princess

This is the song called *Glory in the*
Highest, it has to be loud
It's just about all one note
and we have to hold our mouths right
for this one especially, *Glory*
I'm sorry for the altos
They have to sing O on A
for bars and bars
Karen is the solo, she is a snob

The breathing
is theatrical as all getout
There are almost no crescendoes
We're so loud now
we couldn't make one anyway
Not one of us knows anything about it
but we have to sing in German
and over again in English
translated by Henry S. Drinker:

Wake awake for night is FLAAAAAAH-
ying. The watchman on the height
is CRAAAAAAAH-
ying. It's Cantata No. 140
Wachet Auf by J. S. Bach with an extended
(is it ever) chorale in the middle

Going home in the snow is boring
It's so dry and dark and cold
I am a fabulous robot
We boot the snow and squeak it and shower the others
Karen will tell, she can mind her own beeswax
and just like the dark in summer, spring, and fall
Mom and Dad will do their boring joke

SHADRACH MESHACH AND TOBEDWEGO

The Comet

May I call you sir? after
all, Halley was Sir Edmond,
wasn't he? A knight. But

you, phenomenon, are as follows:
like Appaloosa hide, the meeting
place of Realism *and* Abstraction.

Further, you are an actuary
merely of the Oort Cloud. You are, I
hope to tell you, Pelé. You

are the Christian Science
Monitor. Hairy star, we've
seen the rushes—you're

> potrzebie, you're Peter
> Elbow in the gaudy
> night; many happy
> returns of the day.

A Test

X says to me in his uncanny way,
"Here is how you find me—in these 'tuneless numbers':

$$X = \frac{-b \pm \sqrt{b^2 - 4ac}}{2a} \quad ."$$

He and his ilk are such stereotypes as to speak in more or less
formulaic expressions; but he hides his identity
in my discriminating heart, weak from loss of blood.
"Call me," he says, by way of aftermath. (Pay attention.
This may be a test, real or imaginary.)
His words are a mediation among a) the graphite symbols
in this spiral notebook, and b) human tears, and
c) drops of heart's blood. Let the record show that
X is greater than Pythagoras, and these polynomials will live forever.

1989

"The children who stand alive courageous after the revolution,
they will not resignate" outdoors alone together.
Oversized petites, they rage from zone to zone
in despite of any arrogant polyglot bureaucrat;
their voice is a gazette and frigate, the *Sangre de Cristo,*
in a tenement of principle today on a seacoast in Bohemia full of
    fjordless Vikings.

Curly- or straight-haired responsive incipient grownups
whose scarves are gaskets: the eyes are fissures of men
and women beyond the secular mask, as you might say
Handke, Ramke, Meinke; or Hanema, Brademas, Lertsema.
One Sandy Grimes supplies this stat as colophon:
a career .376 for Louisville; what ho, Harley Street bat—a life
    in any league.

Nature in a setting of its own design
"From crunch underfoot," after centuries
of centuries-old Old-World craftsmanship,
presents the winter of 1989, of Ralph Waldo
Ellison. Coevals in transition, *beaux inconnus,*
you accrue flax and honey, message units, comparable worth, site
    preparation, and the conflicted eustacy of Marbury v. Madison.

A Cookie

Mother drives at eighty-four eighty-four
miles per hour often, despite
cataracts just lifted from her eyes
blue as Route 128 by Dr. St. Clair looking like a rabbit.

Your eyes are beautiful just beautiful he says.
Yes you may drive any time you feel
up to it. I feel up to it she says
all the time and pushing eighty-five she drives

eighty-five easy. I will take a friend
to a daughter's gallery an unnamed friend
from the Chilton Club doing everything like sixty
approaching a cookie by the little butterfly window.

But Drs. St. Clair and Scholl I have floaters
in front of each eye like smut or worms
or *haricots verts* at Mass Eye and Ear
always. They gave a lady a suet muffin.

> I will be receiving the lens implant a week ago last Thursday
> after the cauterization of the occluded region.
> Look at all the fireweed and loosestrife in bloom along
>   Mother Brook
> while I do my utmost to keep my eyes on the road.

Kilim

                A   a
         mammo   pappo
            gram   gram
         hands on hips, feet in stirrups
         indignant (>India? + >ignis)
         haha   hands on hips, *prêt à porter*
What this scarab allows to that ankh, sir,
we are not to know. What effect the isms
         of X or Mohammed or the Buddha
had and/or have (for that matter) on or in
         the flat motif of kilim rugs
we are not to know, but it's not abstract:

                A   at
            Gany   Runny
            mede   mede
sporting a bedspread or a soccer-coach costume
with a half-line in the half-light with a half-life

A lion   swiftly   still
         soars   and stands   so
a tree   high   still
         of life   and wide   soars

Meanwhile, back at the oasis, the ecstatic ones
partake of desert dessert, by the dignified drama dairy

Nashotah

Several people from Chelsea, seminarians and clergy,
in the wand of the Oxford Movement transported to America,
made their way out to the territory, out to Wisconsin,

and up the Root River, full of *racines* and so named therefor,
to build the Red Chapel (1842) and the Blue House (1844)
on the bank of Upper Nashotah Lake. The place was called
   the Mission,

Nashotah Mission. The idea was to baptize
the Oglala Sioux by total immersion.
They looked at the world through horn-rimmed spectacles.

The glacier ground this lake and others
as it gouged through the prairie in Paleozoic time.
But who would name a town after the bottom of a lake?
   Fond du lac?
They sang the Holy Office around and around the calendar.
The idea was to train priests of the Lord
after the order of Melchizedech.

They said, "Offer it up," over and over. Then, they offered it up.

"Mr. Kemper, today is Thursday.
You are to read the morning service in Green Bay
on Sunday. I suggest that you start walking."

To Celeriack Skinner

Dearest gadget, to him I
wrote, thank you for skinning
rabbit food and for Mayo

Clinic. Oldest implement,
I continued, but no longer
did he attend. Rusted and cheery

he was now, knew of some
Ology. He'll to the Mousse Home
go. And seaside, old pot.

The Deer

Here is the deer in the middle of the postcard
picture with his head down and very fancy
very dramatic and sentimental and deserving
a Tiepolo kind of sky over the dominical head

putting his greasy venison onto our table
—the platter's so heavy to lift
it takes two of us to do it

There isn't any drastic color in the winter
You get oldness when you look out
You get reliance on something but what?
in the roads particularly and when the light is going

and you see maybe the frayed fibers
—the postcard is good rag paper—
are deer hairs in a funny-looking
fan or clump or whatever it is

right at the sharp distinctive edge
you couldn't mistake and don't you forget
guilty as blazes in the dark
as if you could be the photographer

Gorbachev Moon

Gorbachev Moon, the red template of a
sickle in the jazzy spheres.

Take off the top of this
distinctive hand-crafted item.
Inside this idea
there is another idea.
To whom does this
idea belong? and that one?
Are there animals in the moon?

Sir, the moon is made of green cheese.
The secular apple of populism beans us all.
I will paint your name on the egg of obverse earth.

Itasca

It thinks you're a tree because
it perceives an
itinerary in your surfactants, but
it will not leave off eying
its prize, the left knob of your collarbone.

It is connected with Rose Macaulay through Mrs. Conybeare.
It seems to say, "I see men as trees walking."

It offers
its copy of *archy* and *meh-*
itabel to
Itzak Perlman.
It has a profound word by way of name.

It's time to acknowledge that
it has a frequent-flyer ticket someone gave
it to take
itself to
Itasca, but
it can't use
it because
it has this practice of clinging constantly to you.

Famous Bigshots

Famous bigshots of the world unite
in black tie and nutria stormcoats,
omnicompetent, handsome dreamboats
totally snazzy and slightly snobby
exclusive hotshots with prodigious bankrolls
for clandestine bombshells, gaslight escorts,
splendidly outfitted armfuls of cashmere
adjudged diaphanous. Old blister,
old beano: auspicious dearies
and snooded consorts, fiscal eggheads
and erstwhile tightwads eleemosynary
to the luscious amanuensis.
With brass putter, vermeil niblick,
bronze mashie and deco Ronson,
footed salver with deckled message,
hammered flask and acajou stick;
with great hat! grand leghorn—these foxy moderns—
      crafty sophisticates,
putative expatriates—they leave their unread half-calf first
edition of *Trilby* by George du Maurier
on the faux-malachite plinth, and they scarpa.
This is a true account of famous bigshots.
Not one word has been distorted or omitted.

Knaves

Knaves behold the Iditarod on TV.
Four white mittens attempt to access the crunchies.
Morgan is making *fondue celestine*.
What's the sentence that's supposed to come next?

I am a painting in view of my green face.
The chattels are vindicated to the fisk.
(Towns which consider, always render themselves.)
Even children can make rose-headed nails.

Waldemar Antimony, a blacksmith, told me this.
A gathering of elders transpires in the kiva.
Mr. Rathbone reads ALL of "Lycidas."
Nina is a famous dentist in St. Louis.

October Poem

October Poem: the sun eclipsed
with your Canada geese again,
their voice a folk not a court instrument.

Swans are their white mirror on the lake or sky,
but even if these geese were walking fish
coambulating on the brittle planet
among the aforesaid, with their ecological honks,
nobody could catch them. They would uphold

the artificial order as ghosted characters
against the clouds like a herringbone jacket.
Days your eyes follow the oblique, slubbed sky.
Nights your bones are cushioned by goslings and cygnets,

transition markers in an ambiguous world,
like the lion abroad, who seems to be drinking
the swans and geese, but they go right on flying
as the surface smooths again. This amounts
to the Augustan formation now in overlay,
as "entertaining, beautiful, and finally important":
Lyon, Fish & Swann—a firm of advocates for poets.

The Secular Mask

Call with Stevens the roller of big cigars
and also those who wealthily to wive
in Padua come, incumbent and erstwhile czars,
and Jerry Garcia *et Paul et Virginie.*
Then "Even in Arcadia we thrive—
ourselves are made of Dedham pottery,"
clatter the twenty-eight, for envious Time
has disgustingly filmed the chandelier with grime.

>I have no code for this, the millennium,
>a gleaming ECNALUBMA up ahead,
>and in the rear-view mirrow Dryden dead
>(whose principals are very much alive—
>from the Clown to the respected Huntress, from
>didactic Venus to allegorical Mars).

Wilma

1. Here is Wilma's poem about what she thought was her
raison d'être.

SONG

Mornings meseems I apprehend the mist of the jellied pole.
Maybe I applicate some beauty. You are talking to myself
　　occluded
until the approach of the recondite veiled functionary on
　　hoofy Percheron
as the picture of Night, Nortoning self to sleep.

Idiot! if subjectively depressed weel then still objectively
constructive at last look at least to the "disinterested,"
Mr. Hershey Bar Cash Register Wastebasket III in the fiery
　　calendar.
I'm Cajun too, contrapposto and myth-related. My
commission expires September 11, 1991 (a palindrome).

Wilma complies, a true story, she gets
up there and sprints. All day
she brings flags to the rummage.
You think she is the oyster man with little bells.

Put another name on her. She is
township in the roots of a tree.
She is the critiqued sneaker.
This poem is about you, you know.
We are still talking about Wilma.

Now, friend, for a plaid urn or bra
difficult of construction
and a Hungarian hairbrush for the present
a deacon　　a dream of bumpkins

So send me yourself for a while on Interlibrary Loan
That's why we pay our taxes, isn't it?
Or if that don't work out for you, please send me Nancy
    Cunard's book please
to be a bouillon cube in the Hibernian vessel, and
you lie between awe and mirth. *They* allow Nancy Cunard.

2.   A piano was being pushed down the smooth beautiful pavement by young men in uniform overalls. They were pushing it toward a small bandstand affair beside Lake Winnepesaukee, where people were sitting in their chairs waiting for music to begin. There were large, graceful light fixtures trained on the bandstand.

Wilma was hiding inside the piano. There was plenty of room for her medium-sized form, but she was feeling sore as she lay across the strings, which were making ridges in her, dozens of red ridges. She tried to keep still.

Horowitz came out in a friendly way. Everyone stood up (except Wilma); the audience was mostly other pianists, glad of the chance to listen to Horowitz while they were on vacation at The Lake.

The great man, the unexampled figure, sat at the piano. I will play Mozart's very early pieces, he said. You will recognize them. He addressed the piano, but no sound came out, only thuds. Horowitz smiled. I am so apologetic, he said. Another piano will have to be brought. Please. The men pushed the piano up the hill again to the big house.

3.   Adrienne is enjoying the office job. It gives her enough time for the poetry. It keeps her mind, at least that part of it which talks, off Wilma. Do you think Wilma was really her half-sister? The collection of Chinese pots was given to the Museum (which has too many already), and the papers are in Houghton. I'm sure the family was right to do that; not an easy bunch to deal with. I am reading Donne who is even dirtier than I had not remembered. I wonder what he would have thought of natural childbirth.

4. Adrienne did NOT write these.

When Wilma died, we crowded round the brink
of the Ganges, and watched the barrow sink
in the gold and leaden water,
she of the light sandal or sarong.
            Roses rode in curricles,
                and it was ecumenical and long.
The lime proceeded ever to inhibit
the scurvy we would not exhibit.

Such wights as viewed this solstice cried,
Sabrina! Lilith! and inside
                bethought them of no miracles.
All was intentioned for its seamy best,
and we our creeds and curricles had long possessed
                when Wilma died.

5. Mrs. Farley closed her book. All this have I conceived, dears,
and especially Adrienne, that you may hear and benefit. We get
up in the morning, we read or sing, we accomplish what we have
presented to ourselves, we may go to the theater. Fundamentals
firmly laid but quickly lapsing. May you embrace your spring hours
with energy. May color and precision be yours. Now I leave you
who judge best when to do so, hoping that always we come back
to reasonable grounding in that which is ours.

I have a question about gnosticism, said Rachel. That there were
two kinds? One said life is meaningless and we're all going to hell in
a handbasket, therefore let's be terribly good and maybe we won't.
And the other kind said life is meaningless and we're all, etc., so
therefore let's do whatever we feel like as much as we want. Both
groups were missing something?

I think they were, said Mrs. Farley. You have to have balance.
Rachel, you have your fuzzy fringed scarf around your shoulders,
and you wear your running shoes. These twain symbolize balance.
Now you are leaving for the Continent almost at once, as I remain
behind. And you carry balance with you. Do not linger in Belgium.

6. I thought you would like to have this letter that was in
Wilma's things. It is not written to you of course as you know
but to Rathbone her late teacher. You have met him I believe, he
and his wife are both charming people.

Dear Mr. Rathbone,

   We have gotten to Athens finally and I was glad to find your
letters here. I don't know when we are getting to New York because
The Winkle is fired with the notion of going to a little uninhabited
island. I wish I could have a cheeseburger and a Diet Coke. I am all
for l. u. islands, but the food here tastes uniformly of olive oil. Every
other night we have a huge fish *paté*. This was glamorous the first
few times.

   Anyway it is an island called Respos which is owned by one
person and we are going there when we have been to the major
archeological places. The Winkle has been there once to see a
mosaic bathtub. Respos is where awful things happened in myths.
I am accustomed to the destruction of empires and the vastness of
history. What are you doing? I hope lots of reading that you didn't
get to do during school and I hope you fixed your serve. Please give
Mrs. Rathbone my love and tell her I have some illegal plants from
around Carcassonne for her and lots from Greece.

                              Yours sincerely,
                              Wilma

7. ADRIENNE: Here I am as it were a dead fish
                   wrapped up in the *New York Times*
                   and which it's an honor to be wrapped up in
                   the face in its kleenex and the eyes' tears
                   the news, the gumdrops and contact lenses

    RACHEL: Arise and quit your rotten talk!
                   Why do you want to be a dead fish
                   or why do you want me to think you are one

ADRIENNE: Last night we were all eating
pie, three kinds, and listening to
Dinah Shore (love ya love ya Dinah)
when a knock came at the door

I went over and answered it and lo
four men entered dressed in furs, but more
important they were singing
the self-same song as Dinah
I view this as a portent

RACHEL: Now let us
go as once agreed and seek employment
You will be excellent as a secretary
with certain executive privileges. For my part,
I shall become a librarian, a soothing one
Geraniums shall be ever on my desk.
Yet soft! what kinds of pie?

ADRIENNE: Peach and Chocolate Cream and Lemon
Meringue

RACHEL: So be it even as when Dinah sang

8. TO TED

A burst jodhpur for the New Year
from a Catalan engraving, the borders with
General Grant pillars that pretend to be the whole point.
Quinine does something funny and hollow to the backs of
your knees.
In twenty minutes you will be a pond that is boring.
I like to think of you that way; now sit here in horseplay,
odd to others that I have put my mittens on your ears.

Quickly I am moving like candy,
grasping onto the General Grant pillars,
my stiff fingers themselves carabiners, holding

dearly, dearly your filmy trust in me
while Nature broods bosomy, dark, and allegorical
and quickly I am racing
for the shadow is breath or folding or whisker
and I am too late to the grape or wiggle and you have gone.

9.   Adrienne has sent her poem "To Ted" to Ted. It is going to be
difficult for him, seeing how it is difficult for me, who know A. so
well, and seeing how A. is not too clear about poem herself! I wish
she would go to poem school and find out how. I know Ted will
show the poem at the shop. He is reliable, but he will be so proud
of being sent poem about him that he will show it to the Grease
Monkeys who will be vile about it and that will get back to A. as
she glides up in whatever car she has relieved parents of, such as the
Saab with the bookbinding interior. And they the Grease Monkeys
will say foul things and A. will go into a remorseful depression like
the summer school one. I wish she had not sent poem to Ted,
because when the chips are down it is you and I, precious Rachel,
and (when she feels like it) Augusta, who will pick up the pieces.
I am eating a stale bagel and it feels like I'm eating a geode.

10.   Dear Adrienne,
   Thank you for the poem. I read it lots and lots and I don't
understand it much but it is beautiful. Can you go to the beach
Sun. I will call. Mr. Rathbone has coughed up a job like last year.
I will do the grounds and paint and this time you will be my
assistant heh heh. I will call. Ted. Heh heh.

11.   …Adrienne and Ted were at the dedication of Wilma's library.
They had been dancing all night at Ephemera and were acting
"close." Ted gave everyone what he calls The Subtle Wink. Some
pals of his whom Rachel says are the Grease Monkeys sang at the
dedication—oh, a lot of things happened that would have made
Wilma laugh, such as her family going around giving everyone their
harried but gorgeous profiles. There was a huge prayer about books.
Mr. Rathbone read ALL of "Lycidas." It really was fun, being out-
doors, everybody could get away from everybody else. Mrs. Farley,

you will be surprised and glad to know, handed out sandwiches and kept her mouth shut.

I must get this in the mail and zip to work, dear Monsignor; please write soon and tell me about le printemps as it appears in Brussels and about all you are doing.

Sincerely yours,

Augusta Fahnestock

12.   Rachel Dear,

I am sorry not to welcome you myself with proverbial open arms to Las Cruces, but after many hoos and haaas I have been admitted to the Argentine group with the Peace Corps and (my letter to Clain explains all) told to get on a plane. I offer you my teapot as the engagement present. It is under the green sofa in the living room, and in two years when I get back I will have your name put on it. I can't tell you how happy I am for you both.

What I envy you perishing Yankees is your shade trees and you will see that I have been busy from time to time getting some ranch shade when Clain takes you around. The pines worked out. One of the places I like to go is back in the creek backpools—it is so pretty there. I hope you will like all of it. I will send you a piece of art from the S.A. wilderness which they tell me has no name.

With love from Elizabeth Guthrie.

13.   And here is Stanton Rathbone's stilted and opaque poem to the purported memory of Wilma, if you can get through it.

OUR LADY OF GUACAMOLE

While captains of industry select a theme from the Zeitgeist
and run it into the ground, while fundamentalists
of any stripe validate what they feel like thinking
in atavism, so here in these unrhymed
cinquains, there's nothing of the kind.

The oldest poem definitely written in French
is the "Sequence of Saint Eulalia" (843).
It opens, *Buone pulcele fut Eulalie,*
an analogue, as balladmongers will tell you.
of "Frankie Was a Good Girl." It's in quatrains, not in cinquains.

"What the Scripture omitteth must be supplied by our charitable
imagination," if you believe the pseudo-Bonaventure,
some history-buff sacristy rat in swearing-type sanctuary
reds, who dreamt of rolfing his subject and mine,
which, nardlike and cross-cultural, is Mary the Mother of Jesus.

In 1959 I was standing in a church in Paris
supposedly looking at architecture with Margaret
Rowe, Curator (Emerita) at the time
of Laces and Fans at the Yale Museum of Art
(229 Chapel St., New Haven, Connecticut),

and directly in front of us was a hefty tablet
which read: "Here lie the horrible Catholics
who were slain by the glorious Huguenots," and Professor Rowe
cried COME WITH ME and marched me around the corner
to a nearly identical monument whose tablet

read: "Here lie the horrible Huguenots/Who were slain
by the glorious Catholics." This anecdote stands
as subtext. The Venus de Milo (who has waived
the right to bare arms, in a manner of speaking
[these arms are held in escrow somewhere]) we also saw that year

or the next, with somebody else: a squilgy of recollection.
Aloha, Bona Dea, aloe vera in the psychoceramic biobit.
Yet who was the Stabat Pater? Rinehart? Mr.
Jones of Jesus, decorated and perpendicular?
Aloha, Balm of Kuviasunggnerks and Eisteddfodds

whom we identify as a female role model in binomial
    nomenclature
on one hand the Madonna of the Environment
    (Vâche-sur-Lune)
and on another the (dicy) Venus of Willendorf and
on a third hand (gulp) Diana of the Ephesians
in a democratic configuration along the lines of the Trinity.

Lead us not into Penn Station, nor the late Ohrbach's
    or Altman's,
neither into the Pierpont Morgan Library (parallel structures)
(westering, you can take in the Shrine of Walsingham
in Sheboygan, Wisconsin, [which turns our Episcopalian,
however]), virtually snockered by the handles:

Holy Folklorico Moly! *ark at er lovey*:
Sainte Marie de Ratatouille Niçoise, the (Recusant)
Virgin of Killiecrankie, Our Lady of (of
all things) Guacamole, *ora pro* whomsoever,
steady on, Notre Dame de Folding Chairs.

14. …Rachel has been staying with Mrs. Farley, and reports that
she (Mrs. F.) looks like Batman in a cape and that lunch and dinner
are watercress avocado port du salut cheese and such. Mrs. Farley is
getting bad eyes so Rachel or other transient reads *Northanger Abbey*
to her. Rachel sez it is great in NA when the girl thinks she has
found a secret document in the castle and it turns out to be a laun-
dry list. Mrs. Farley corresponds with Mrs. Guthrie as you might
expect. Mrs. F. thinks she will visit Mrs. G. in the Argentine, which
would be ghastly for all if you ask me, which no one has. Mrs. F.,
mindful through books of an India that was and isn't, and confusing
that India with Argentina, thinks of chiffon and fans and stuff
which Mrs. G. would denounce as rot, or why did she go there.
Adrienne's poems are more and more published in nice mags. One
is called *Parsnip Wine*.

Later. Do you honestly believe she is a reincarnation of Wilma. Don't worry about it. I don't believe any of that stuff. Mrs. Guthrie's material about Argentina is becoming a book, wowser, under a different name. I mention this because of something downright peculiar. The Indians (not what they are) there seem to know about Wilma. They think she is some sort of spirit, and they know all about Mr. Rathbone, whom most people are trying to forget. Ask Monsignor…

15.   THE OCCLUDED SULTRY

sandpiper of single throat
keewilli keewilli Ruskin Carlyle
my lady the last best beautiful

dreamer, toes are wet in waves
that sigh away from her
till she stirs and wakes and sighs
where is the General I know
here a short sleep ago in the sands

where is he of single throat
mon général and in your toes and sweet
sideburns General Grant! whispering to you
that the sandpiper is the secret bearer
and envy of the wave, here I am

Which *Parsnip* will print. Rachel, I am thinking about Wilma. Ted too. We have gone over all the papers over and over and the letters. Mrs. Guthrie sent loads of stuff. Ted has got maps pasted all over the boathouse walls and darling little pins with pointed flags on them. And a chart saying what it means. Tonight we spent packing the car with the essentials. We think we can find her.

A Rune

As I in *baden-zuyt* was entreating stop-and-go Pushkin here around
the dubious greensward (Hopkins, Brockles, and Chippy *in articulo
mortis*), was I ever bonkers from the experience. Bons coeurs I was.
Took place entirely in the sack of sphagnum. Took place on the
slats with clone of Indigo Jones. Ottonian bricklayers "forgot" how
to lay brick. You might take one of them for a Lally column, and I
will Charleston with him (watch it that you do not sideswipe the
Briggs-Copeland incumbent). Then grrrr, he picks up a Hamill
Wedge, and where does that leave me? The HW is gravity flow, by
design. "Clean wet dog around house runs, indignant at bath"; loses
weight in Amish Country, as against this.

And as I was pronto and presto putting Quinquireme of
Nineveh and other prerequisites and emollients on the proper *com-
plexioun*, Nerd Mass at 5 P.M. (sensitive pastoral—even the priest is
a nerd), oyster stew 6, and then pool (and pool poem) at .004 knots.
Got lifeguard, Chris (not his real name), to do the math. Don some
laundry—"Lord Raglan." Pushkin chomps the blefescue.

I write you parenting anyhow from Rhode Island and Providence
Plantations, which is patently half under water; and what *I* want to
know is, there's a chop in the fingerbowl (pathetic fallacy), why
don't they move the Indy to the Astrodome? Will you guys please
row the damned Grand Rapids boat ashore? Making Orphic-type
music out of dead pieces of tree and old tusks: Sigmund Romberg.
So please burn this now—OK?

Coffee Table Book

1. Coffee

> Mary has a lexical appreciation
> of all the beautiful varieties of coffee you can buy.

> "The dry leaves smell like curry powder."
> It was the most evocative sentence he had recently heard.

> Now the tape is going on the player, Mississippi
> John Hurt singing "Coffee Blues."
> The volutes of her heart are stirring.

2. Table

> On the coffee-colored corridor wall is a nineteenth-
> century diagram of the Periodic Table.

> On the turntable the sounds are circulating
> now, on and on, oh elegiac Mary.
> A book's her mantilla, for correct posture.

3. Book

> Oh, glossy blue vellum, royal fancy exterior!
> textile of the text, gospel of Mary!

> Oh, Viking predators would rip that
> cover right off! if it were the Dark Ages.
> Oh, prints of the blood! *William* Hurt! Gore Vidal!

> But the he of the poem swirls the coffee in his cup,
> saying, "Mary, my dear, I'd throw the book at 'em!"
> The table of contents speaks volumes, validating the cliché.

Reverse Painting

This then is the end then, isn't it, the purpose
the anagram which we are destroying
This is the cipher, lads, to solve
the knock-knock on an epiphany
This is the rebus of the hour, such a pain
This is the palindrome which someone
took notes for, night shadows
This is the protective glass through which our glance
passes and receives enlightenment
as an eye looking out at us
which it is

To Newfoundland

1989

The Stone Calendar

The personnel of January are standing
stones with two traditional faces.

Faces that are the lard and cinders
of February. I was watching them there

where the moon of March lit them
and behold they said they were cold

yet not so cold in April as
previously. Further, there were pleasant

side-effects such as the expected May flowers
which put some slight blush there on them

which fulminated, inasmuch as it became
June. So they mopped their brows

in July too. Pah! in August with
quadrants of leafy faces. Only

in September they with tempered
relief rest in tawny shade, with

dolor too for the October nasty
winds and November more follow.

So there they ever are almost back where they
began in December looking at the chilly prospect.

Beach Poem

This poem proceeds matter-of-factly up from the basis
of particulars, hidden element, deliberate
premises of sandpipers' amusing feet, occupationally
cold, but they like it like that, they don't mind a bit

and this here bird digresses from other patterers
as the current stanza diverges if only slightly
in the expensive lenses of uncomfortable muffled birdwatchers
luminous girder-colored lumps on sticks

The streets of the New World are paved with broken gasp
glass the shards of the Industrial Revolution
but naturally mellowed out by constant whacking and sifting

Hence will you not walk on the topos of previous perishing
literary remarks about mortality and mutability?
on this moratorium of stone and water?
the combers are hyper and if you'll forgive me navy blue

and hollow and bright. Leaving weirdo interesting
striped horizontal grittings in the somewhat severe
arenaria groenlandica. This last upholds a kind of compact
with the vegetable; the mineral I've sufficiently touched on.

Background

A Poem in Envy of Baudelaire

I want a canvas boudoir pinked with runes
where I can belt out mannerist broadsides evincing me
at sea in the sky, so my neighbors will consist of bells
and the wind will blow their religious bongs in my dreams.
I will thus note the alfresco phenomena of Victorian
optimism's urban obelisk and cylinder or whatever
with my mopish chin in my hands.
                     For what I ask you
could be more divine than the cocktail hour's
four nightlights: Venus, but also my gooseneck lamp,
the Hudson River School of the Aurora Borealis
up and down the firmament. Fourth, the adulated moon's dispatch
of pale enchantment. Ditto spring summer fall
and monochromatic winter as who should know. I'll blanket
myself in textiles thank you and muffle
in the spongecake monoliths of Las Percales.
At this I'll dream all the pedagogic baggage
of Western Civ: provincial ballparks, provisionally
morphic blue horizons at length and smoochings,
symbolic birds sounding off around the clock and other earmarks
of the leftovers of the bombast and piffle of Courtly Love.
Thus Prince in all sorts of positive and negative and actually
neutral Nature experiences or at least impressions of same
it's business at usual. Disguised, the storm will roar
and the image I'm getting is highly well maybe this isn't
what you talk about but ecstatic and closely allied to determining
some sort of climate of stability from burning issues if you take me.

Pantoum du chat

Charles and I go out together
in his boat, which is a cat-
amaran, in the burnishing weather,
elated, so it's not surprising that

in his boat, which is a cat
at top speed among cats, this poem begins.
Elated, so it's not surprising that
we sing "Speed Bonnie Boat" to the winds.

At top speed among cats, this poem begins
making me seasick. "This malady," says Charles, "will become,
as we sing 'Speed Bonnie Boat' to the winds,
as naught," preventing them from

making me seasick. "This malady," says Charles, "will become
the narrative wave of the future, the wave of metaphor,
the wave of Narragansett Bay, of foam.
All the clichés for cats: liquid, longueur, languor,

the narrative wave. Of the future: the wave of metaphor,
I say, will be transfigured by the cat.
All the clichés for cats: liquid, longueur, languor,
as among poems this wave begins that

I say will be transfigured by the cat
as the cat leaps, you know, in timely weather."
All this of course in a Catamaran Voice, the times that
Charles and I go out together.

Give Me an A

Give me an A
A capital
as Dürer made A and D his own

A calls the other letters
in all the languages
come here   come here
Q peculiar   necessary U
roll me over R and steadfast I
says A

and cheered or grumbling
bumping up against each other
getting out of line becoming words
and lining up they're characters

Railroads and Newspapers

As we rode the Chicago Milwaukee St. Paul and Pacific
Railroad we read the paper—the *Chicago Sun-Times* and the
    Minneapolis Tribune,
recalling that on the New York New Haven and Hartford of blessed
    memory it used to be terrific

to read the *New Haven Register,* the *Hartford Courant,* and the
    Times, prolific
as we were. Then we rode the Chesapeake and Ohio and
    pretty soon
out the window we saw some rolling stock from the Chicago
    Milwaukee St. Paul and Pacific.

During this leg of what turned out to be a trip we read the
    Cleveland Plain Dealer and the *Detroit Free Press*—the funnies,
    to be specific.
Then we rode the tiny, arcanely distinguished Detroit and
    Mackinac Railroad and the moon
rose over the Lower Forty-Eight, sentimental and honorific.

If Ic
arus had ridden the rails in his hybristic noon,
the Chicago Milwaukee St. Paul and Pacific

Railroad would have been his dish of tea. Diffic
ult to imagine. Under the obituary page of the *New Orleans*
    Times-Picayune
we slept editorially, such thoughts being soporific;

yet at which point the locomotive up ahead exploded in a fiery
blue crash and we were all killed instantly (and signific
    ant people promptly read about it in the *Chicago Sun-Times* and
    the *Minneapolis Tribune*)
on the Chicago Milwaukee St. Paul and Pacific
Railroad, a fur piece from the late New York New Haven and
    Hartford. What a wonderful outfit that was. Wasn't it terrific.

A Song for Saint Cecilia's Day 1987

Cecilia will always play
the organ
with her galoshes on
so she
can
hit more notes that way.
Laryngitis is her
nemesis.
Stuffed under her misericorde is a
scrumptious roman à clef
involving Bliss Carman and Blossom Dearie
to read on breaks during this frequent ad-hoc get-together.

Frank's Drum Shop off Adams
Street in the Loop supplies
the Zildjian cymbals and the Ludwig drums
for the occasion. The shaggy drummer cries,
"Today
we had an outdoor
Chem class. You can have more
explosions that way."

Then beer and wine and Coke
(innocuous, low-octane grog) and scads of food
which no one would
show up without, appear:
kielbasa and onions
roasted the way they are
in the streets of Warsaw on Saint Cecilia's Day.
Hot mushrooms stuffed with themselves and scallions,

somebody's mysterious, rich standby—tortellin
i and lima bean
salad with hearts of artichoke.
This actually tastes really good.
The trumpeter is an introvert whose might and ardor
Chris
topher Hogwood's dis
tinguished biography of Handel touches on, this
"singular idea or *Affekt*"
in the candid blasts and bore
of said trumpeter's snaky cuspidor.

"I'm certainly glad I never took up the
violin," said a
cellist invented by John
Ashbery and James Schuyler in *A Nest of Ninnies.*
"It's so confusing
not to have something
to lean on."

This remark might just
have been made by the cellist of record in his slump
of severe
orthopedic difficulties,
which don't somehow interfere
with the timing
of the august,
deliberate indecisiveness
of his gorgeous, triumph
alistic lows.

The two fiddlers are his buddies
and roomies.
Not much is known about either one
by anybody, because they say little and that in unison,
believing

that everything
is pretty OK and great
and so are in a position to concentrate.

All scowling five males are of course spaced out
on the girl flutist
whose sufficient blond ponytail shines
beyond the silver flute,
but only one of them is sleeping
with her—it's the drummer. They
haven't told anybody about it. Weeping
seeds of little tears, sighs for the recent curve of
the drummer's sweaty back, if we only knew,
all for love
(toward the others she's a Platonist);
but off goes the flute narrative now concerning divers pearls
of dryads, Naiads, and such-
like girls and in triads, huge
and various Deist
ically oriented Papist
subterfuge,
much as "care
less and dar
ing" Miss Mar
gar
et Bryant calls Dryden's stan
zas, in the Eleventh Edition (1911) of the Encyclopedia
Britan
nica.

Music, as Auden not too long
ago observed, does not smell,
while John Russell
in the *Times* more recently said:
"Cherubim
open their mouths wide in compulsory song,"
by way of doxology,

and we should hark to him as well.
Artful Cecilia clomps the sacred premises,
and all the whiffling bellows to produce the notes is made
from old Electroluxes in a variation on a Rube
Goldberg arrangement. The whole thing gets taped
for the net and tube.

Lizzie Borden Through Art
and Literature

Somewhat to the east of East Providence, driving along 195,
the USS Massachusetts rides at (permanent) anchor
in the brackish river-harbor of Fall River
(her sister the Constitution further to the north
in the Bay Colony slapping similarly).
Myth once there (in 1892, Clio in abeyance), cruel and untrue as it
    turned out,
sprang full blown from the old brow of the coast-to-coast
    newspaper-swallowing populace!

> Bright leavings of hammers Elizabeth Borden grasped,
> much as was Carthage blitzed, or Egypt asped,
> to whose male parent-unit to administer
> buffets twoscore revealed in quatrain sinister.
> Which when the principal looked upon amain,
> the surrogate womb full forty shee againe.

The original manuscript as it were a palimpsest,
since the "piece" is the instant art of oral-formulaic illiterate
    tradition

featuring 1) formulas, 2) incremental repetition, 3) the single epic
    hero in conflict with the dark adversary, 4) abrupt juxtaposition
    instead of subtle transition;
but it hardly stopped there. Ballets danced for her (acquitted in a
    court of law) guilt,
clouded subsequent recollections of impeccable statespersons,
celluloid spent, dazzling and mock-heroic tours-de-force of
    New Faces and the Kingston Trio,
good reads, and sensible histories of the Industrial Revolution.

Exploring Unknown Territory

Exploring unknown territory wearing Admiral Peary's earflaps
is a moot beginning to a metaphysical poem.
There doesn't seem to be an explanation of how the poet came into
    the possession of the earflaps
or any particular virtue to them that could rub off on the poet and
    make her or him soar in realms of blue.

Admiral Peary would probably not have countenanced the blue
    movie or *Fear-of-Flying*-type books,
not that he was attracted to "realms of gold" either.
But it is quite in order to lie, to steadfastly present an explanation of
    the earflaps,
as if it were just what had happened, making the reader totally
    comfortable.

∞∞∞

One of the important points in Boethius from a stylistic, not
philosophic, point of view, is that in the great length of *The
Consolation of Philosophy,* and in the subtle structure, with its
poignant emotional steps, he alternates passages of verse and prose.
The variety and multiplicity of the universe is its joy as well as its
puzzlement. Boethius knew this well. This is a leaf out of his book.

∞∞∞

My husband, who is probably my best critic,
is not absolutely sure whether Peary discovered the South or North
    but believes it was the North Pole.

∞∞∞

ADMIRAL PEARY: Millicent has fine hands and firm, creamlike skin.
MY HUSBAND: Is Millicent a relative?
ADMIRAL PEARY: Well, yes and no.

MILLICENT:	Here are the earflaps. The band fits snugly over the headpiece, and then the strap goes under the chin, so.
MY HUSBAND:	I hope you have a splendid trip. I must say I rather wish I were going with you. Goodbye, sir.
ADMIRAL PEARY:	Goodbye.

ooooo

Documentation of sources: a weary time, a weary time. Some kind of freshening, of loosening of the sensibilities is necessary, sort of what Boethius did, in order to constantly make the connection between the source (*fons*) of the information, and the conclusions gathered (*electa*) from the information. How is the material presented? The process of documentation can be very exacting.

ooooo

Dear Sir,
Please send me a pair of earflaps identical with the ones you sent me in March of 1907. I have found these handsome and serviceable.
Yours very truly,
Admiral Peary.

ooooo

MY HUSBAND:	Have you looked up Admiral Peary?
I:	No, I was busy. Does Millicent bother you at all?
MY HUSBAND:	No, I think she's lovely. But I really believe that it is one-sided to write about Boethius and not write about Isidore of Seville.

ooooo

I don't know what you think you will find. I think it is dangerous and stupid to go away like that. I think you should be careful about charts. The scar on your foot will be recognized as you enter cities. You will have dreams again whenever you go away. It is a great risk.

ooooo

MY HUSBAND: Mr. Ashbery, would you look at my poem?

JOHN ASHBERY: Sure. (Reads aloud.)

One of the Nice Things About Winter
by Mason Knox
The garbage cans don't smell
And nothing grows in them no more.
Now you read one of mine.

MY HUSBAND: Thank you. (Reads silently.) But this is full of French!

JOHN ASHBERY: They aren't the same poem.

MY HUSBAND: Why do you say you write romantic poems and not metaphysical poems? It seems to me that if you write poems that are commenting on themselves as they are being written and read, that's about as metaphysical as you can get.

JOHN ASHBERY: Ah! you are saying that the earflaps prevent hearing!

MY HUSBAND: The earflaps?

ooooo

A picaresque adventure. My husband and I are twenty and nineteen, respectively. It is some time ago. We are walking down Main Street in Stonington, Connecticut, from his parents' house to his grandmother's house. We have blocks of wood and sandpaper in our hands which we are sanding down so that we can paint Russian Orthodox icons on them. A lady is sitting in an upstairs window of one of the houses. She says to someone in the room, "There goes that stupid Mason Knox and his stupid girlfriend doing something stupid again."

ooooo

ADMIRAL PEARY: Welcome aboard, sir.

JOHN ASHBERY: Thank you, but I will not come aboard. I am quite happy here.

ADMIRAL PEARY: But you'll freeze.

JOHN ASHBERY: I won't freeze. Before you left, did you see Mason Knox?

ADMIRAL PEARY: Well, yes. He was in New York. He was reading a paper.

JOHN ASHBERY: How was he?

ADMIRAL PEARY: Fine.

∞∞∞∞

ADMIRAL PEARY: What is this?

G. M. HOPKINS: This is the random grim forge. I wrote about it in "Felix Randal."

ADMIRAL PEARY: I don't see why it's random.

G. M. HOPKINS: John Ashbery does not write metaphysical poems.

ADMIRAL PEARY: Oh. What is the forge doing here.

G. M. HOPKINS: Ashbery would say it was part of the documentation. I am willing to give him that.

∞∞∞∞

MY HUSBAND: Now that you've blown our cover, I suppose you will put Admiral Peary's earflaps on the Russian Orthodox icon.

I: No. Here comes Mr. Ashbery.

JOHN ASHBERY: (Very quietly, to my husband; we are at a large, elaborate party.) I have done some poems involving Isidore of Seville's *Etymologies*. In this work he gives a great many false etymologies of words and concepts, but the etymologies are only a pretext for presenting volumes of information that he wanted to get across anyway.

MY HUSBAND: You don't have to tell me about old Isidore. I'm a canonist.

JOHN ASHBERY: No kidding. Then would you please explain this parchment to me.

MY HUSBAND: Sure, I'll try.

∞∞∞∞

I have a college classmate who is an expert in the care of decaying documents. During the Venetian flood she worked for CRIA and saved many treasures by wonderful methods. She wrote and said we should roll out the parchment as though it were piecrust. Then we should tack it lightly all around the edges, and iron it at a low setting. She says we have to be very careful with the ink.

ooooo

MY HUSBAND:	Which parchment?
I:	Well, it isn't parchment. The part about John Ashbery was a dream-vision, that's all.
MY HUSBAND:	For God's sake, what is it then?
I:	Xerox paper. I got it out of the wastebasket. It has a little printing on the other side.—It's very difficult about the ending.
MY HUSBAND:	I don't see why.
I:	Well, in any normal thing you write, you say what you think you've discovered, and you repeat why you wanted to get into it in the first place. You finish with a mush sentence—thus we see that Walker and Jones (1976) could not fail to conclude, *etc.*
MY HUSBAND:	I wish you would end with Millicent.
I:	That's not a bad idea.

ooooo

MILLICENT:	First, I take the cream cheese, softened, and beat in the sifted flour and baking powder.—There's someone at the door.
ADMIRAL PEARY:	Millicent? Millicent my dear.
MILLICENT:	You're back! Extraordinary! Everyone will be delighted!
ADMIRAL PEARY:	Get your things.
MILLICENT:	What? Right now?
ADMIRAL PEARY:	Right now. We're going over to the Smithsonian.

Log of the Snow Star

Chief asked if I'd go aloft, and in spite of boots
and other impedimenta I said yes
and went. The lower shrouds are easy and over
the top you go and then begins a single
line of ratlines. Tilberry right behind me,
so I said You go on ahead, and this he did.

Then Tilberry handed me the gasket
and Pedersen said to put it through, in fact.
Look LOOK said Tilberry there's corposants.

What's got into this old grump. From his nails
from the spars, the dull light, the legend in hand:
St. Elmo's Fire. We didn't say it was.
Where did Tilberry get it. We didn't
say anything into the sky, bright before snow.

Then climbed down slowly but not so slowly
as to hold up Tilberry, who was climbing down
above me. Chief came out and called us
as for coffee. Made chafing gear on watch.
Learned Swedish profanity from Chips, who tried
to kiss me. Christine and I that night
also out on the jibboom; but up on the fore
t'gallant yard the schooner the *Snow Star*
is her own sailing model in the wand of minor planets.

The Heart

Send the First-Amendment Heart (to the showers glistening)
on the Fifth-Amendment Sleeve as it were a corporate ensign

logo PDQ back to me. For the figural
witness which I floated is not more cost-effective

than principle and we ought to remain
Brown v. Board of Ed. about problem-solving

in any (hapless) event. I'll as a floral summat receive it *a capella*
home, hardly artillery, as some. Now so far

heart, flag, and rose, *res publica,* the bower,
the expected to take seriously. The thorny

pillow is furled in the bosom of the legislature
(what a dicy GRE and the mirror of a Hasselblad

at this writing. Apocalyptic condescends to allegory, believe us,
so wartish bombastic don whose throwaways are foregrounded).

Tassels and all affixed, load ammo rebate FOB
with Hu-Kwa up in Audi, *avoir du poids* of oxgang;

but I'll take the Fifth, bolting from League to League;
"The silken veil of crystal is the closest

thing to nothing between your lips and the wine."
That's what they tell me anyhow in Peoria
and Pawtucket regardless, in a *Doppelgänger* of capillary action.

To Newfoundland

Rural poverty makes for maritime enterprise, they say. This is why over and over ships from Scandinavian ports left for the New World, manned by many men and dogs. You can imagine that the circumstancs of a) being tempest-tossed and blown off course while trying to get to Greenland, and b) missing Greenland altogether, and c) discovering Newfoundland, were an occasion for quantities of poetry writing by those involved. Some of the poetry was terrible and highly inaccurate. Few have the gift. Here are examples:

DOGS: Bough! Wough! whose dogs are we
whan al our maysters are frae hame
or off to Greenland on the sea

We hae nae laird   We have no lord
We all are equal in this place
Bough! Wough! the glancing chop
betides wi' froth the lop-eared face

In curragh rough or beamy knarr
the crew are all impressed
and row beside the Newfoundland dogs
to Newfoundland in the West

Let cairns rain down upon ye
bearing petroglyphs
Let ogham be in your ears
Let there be mastiffs

VIKING CAPTAIN: Maybe we will emulate (and not tell the priest)
Radwald the Wuffing our distinguished cousin
He received Christ but held on tight
to all the old gods just in case

I have to speak in quatrains
because I am a protagonist
The things we did were horrifying
but we were brave and they're over with

Farewell to unfair Harald Fairhair
He thinks to unite all the kinglets is grand
He must do it without my historical help
I'm going to Newfoundland

CREW: Tae Aberdour, frae Norrowa
Tae ony place but here
we'll tak the hand-carved artifact
the replica of the spear

We'll tak the powdered reindeer horn
the elvish herbish brume
with kindergarten spindlewhorl
we seek our new-found hame

To Newfoundland, to Newfoundland
with Viking dogs and sleds
with Nordic thought from Tacitus
and helmets on our heads

I chewed up the Captain's bone skates because he didn't let
me go on the inland voyage. I am a strong Newf now and can do
everything that Bladethorpe can do and as fast, and I don't get my
leggings tangled up like he does. Lots of Newves get to go at age
two but not me. The Indian dogs are odd and not particularly
friendly. Their hair is pretty short, perhaps because of poor diet.
Some of us mated with them anyway—that's how it goes. The
settlement is going to be huge and will fill up the valley of
L'Anse-aux-Meadows. It is like a dog dish full of the sea. I chased
some deer off; they can run eleven miles in fifty minutes. The fish-
ing is the absolute greatest, miles of water up to the knees teeming
with salmon and adolescent codfish. I'd just as lief stay forever.

Here's how we operate. The fish swim right up to shore to eat fallen tree blossoms. We hide in packs behind the trees. Suddenly we all charge in and grab them. Every little dog gets his fish. MANY DOGS HERE, we wrote in the sand in our *futharc*, so happy and crammed full of dinner. The master said, "Footing of divers great beasts!"

Bladethorpe is too arrogant; he's the Dream of the Rude. He says that the celebrated dog that met St. Brendan in the New World was a Bladethorpe of Bladethorpe Newfie. Anyone who believes that Brendan stuff is crazy. Bladethorpe has a little blanket made of *wadmal*. It is so effete but he's into it; the starboard watch confided all this to me. He Bladethorpe also thinks that the Beothuk Indians are related to Beowulf. What an idiot.

There was a Great Auk roast in a grove of hackmatack with games beforehand, poetry afterward. It was part of The Thing. Several Beothuk came and in an "amicable gesture" poured seawater over the Master's head. You can bet Bladehorpe saw this as some kind of rite. The Beothuk heaved cornbread at us. To make this, maize is brayed in a mortar, mixed with water into dough, and separated into cakes which are cooked on a hot stone covered with pebbles. The poet was brushing a quadrant of my "peltry." He had scalded himself on the chowder and so was temporarily mute. There is nothing in this world as good as the dog-backrubs given by Thornhild. She is a beautiful woman who stirs puddings in the smelly kitchen. I love to be there—she fluffs my ruff. "If grownup Newfies look like puppies, and they do, what do Newf puppies look like, I ask?" she asked.

I like to participate in Thornhild's life to a degree. She told this provenance of herself. She had had a sweetheart back home who was conscribed to Harald's army. She told him she'd tie back her hair and put on men's clothing and pass as his comrade as they marched along. No one would ever know. Wouldn't he let her go with him (it grieved her heart so, and she said it three times). He said no my love no (*na min leof na*) three times and then gave her his final answer: no my love no. This is how Thornhild came to the New World—to lose lost love. She also learned to cook whelk.

One of the feast day games went like this. Olaf, a sailor, nailed his boots to two barrel-staves. Then he got out in the wake of the (supple, clinker-built) pinnace tied to a line by his middle. He stood up on the barrel-staves and got towed around for hours, flukes spooming fore and aft among the bergs and growlers. Many barks along the coast that day. We observed the swells. Another game was to make oubliettes for caribou.

The bergs are like burgs. They used to be part of the northern glaciers; then the glaciers calved and the bergs came here. The sailors call them "flyaway islands." Birds live on them: ptarmigan, guillemot, merganser, auk, and puffin. I was disgusted to see the trout eat mice! I've eaten a lot of trout. Give me substantial caribou bones any day. I like to chew them up immediately so I can have some nostalgia about them.

There is one more strange thing to tell. The master and our party were sailing along the coast right near and something gleamed. It was a uniped. It came jumping down to the boat and shot an arrow into the very center of the master's heart. He prophesied and later he died. The poet was along and wrote:

> The men were chasing,
> and it is true,
> a uniped
> down to the beach
> This weird creature
> streaked away
> sank in water
> Hear, O ship master!

Thornhild and I did not know what to think of that. Bladethorpe met us when the boat came ashore and told us the names of his children: Grommet, Rage, Bloodthorpe, Toastcruncher, Petit Nord, Main Tempest, Mound, Biffures, Boney's Rescue, The Fractious One. Indian branch: Eskimo Whooper, Boffin of Baffin. The red line of Newfies descends from the Eskimo dogs. Anyway, there you have it—quadruped, biped, and uniped, all pretty much bilaterally symmetrical. Thornhild and I developed Olaf's "theme," splashing around on the beach. She was throwing an oar in for me to fetch. With the oar on this feast day we wrote in the sand what was doubtless in every heart:

THE MORE TERRE

THE LESS NEUVE

Movement along the Frieze

Who are these people who have gotten their grammar and their
    diction levels
the way they want them. Who are their sweethearts
and who is their friend that they call up in McKeesport
and say something to. A plain tale. Please like their work.
Please like what men and women and children present the line-
breaks of. How did they get their act together
in the matter of sentence fragments, which are sacraments,
and of all those Nortony things, in their English-teacher costumes
or barn clothes and out partying in Bayonne, New Jersey, writing
    stuff down all the time.
Please anyway read what they brought out of the despair
of the boringness of expected word order and what got printed
    with margins
on four sides of it, in what somebody else, a graphics person,
figured out for a typeface; oh please like all these
and the cover of paper which is supposed to decompose
so that they will have something to write their elegiac and
    mutability
poems about, some of them even MID-party arguing in oral comma
    splice
that written comma splice is a form of parallel structure
and so not only justified but welcome! and others loudly disagreeing
totally. (And one of the noisiest avers that incremental repetition
is a form of parallel structure!) Some write syntax down goofy
and then go back and put profundity in
—which is fine—in an air of peace and freedom
as some of them have fasted or will fast or otherwise
sacrifice. A trace of movement along the frieze.
"For a symbolic hand," says this one or the other,
"lies on the pulse of protean co-Americans,

the very hand on the light table, the gong's mallet,
an instrument like my word: confusion of stillness
and motion, the *horror vacui,* and the ancient
nobility of fictive farce!" Perhaps, please,
among blot and stipple and among these nattering damned
didactic SAT and vocabulary words, which are boring
or stunning (in exigency of plot as metaphor) sometimes
to read, the poems are honored by your time and attention.

The House Party

1984

I Have Met Freddy

I have met Freddy again in the masterful gazebo.
This time he brought along his collection of marble statues (tiny)
    and he brought Daphne
Petersen who is staying on another three weeks at The Lion because
    the Nantucket people
have not gotten out of her house. The cutest—far and away—statue
is a shepherdess who is taking a thorn out of her charge's foot,
    Androcles-like,
and it is quite unornamented, unlike the others, which are tartishly
    polychromed.
Daphne was saying that terry cloth is a good bet for the—then we
    were interrupted by

birds! flinging themelves against the vines! madly trying to get into
    the gazebo.
Not understanding what was happening, we all three took fright,
    although pretending to be amused.
Daphne annoyingly fled into Freddy's arms, which were trying to
    fend off such birds as had penetrated the netting,
and while he was extemely flattered by Daphne's "advances," which
    really were advances,
he was also terribly peeved at having to do so many things at once.
Suddenly all the birds went off to bash into something else, and
    Daphne unwound her cashmere hands with silvery-pink long
    fingernails from around poor brave Freddy's neck,
and a few birds that were left clutched rather faintly at the inside
    netting, wanting out again after all that.
Daphne and I picked up all the marble figures and wrapped them in
    their tissue paper and put them back in the box.

Freddy said that if he had been any kind of anything at all he would have brought one of those walking sticks that has brandy secretly inside, and you screw off the head and quaff with your friends, and then you suggest that everybody walk down to the out-buildings and look at the new baby pigs born last week, they are doing so well.

The Fat Baby

the fat baby is in her own thought
she is rocked on her self
she is her basket

her fingers make a star for themselves
around anything

a rabbit is inside her   or is that milk
if milk   how fuzzy

Nancy Drew

Tripping over road apples, we entered the bone orchard for a neck-
 tie party,
duded up in ratcatchers and loaded to the Plimsoll Line
with stool pigeons, polecats, sidewinders, and firewater.
The Smith and Wesson (property of the Nation's Attic) provided a
 leaden powder river (of the National Pastime) past the trembling
 cannon-fodder,
sitting ducks who took a powder in fuzzmobiles to keep their
 powder dry,
hard by wall-to-wall stiffs, poison pens, the numbers game, and
 other war horses and old chestnuts.
Well, the upshot was a rhubarb, a donnybrook, a Chinese fire drill:
gumshoe Roman Policier, eschewing mentor's coke and Strad,
 clapped the bracelets
on Manuel Laboro of uncertain address, and subsequently "twitcht
 his Mantle blue" and amscrayed,
brandishing his bumbershoot and flicking his tufera into the
 cuspidor.

A Poem Beginning with a Line by Wyatt

They flee from me that sometime did me seek
at 2:30 A.M. in the morning tiptoeing around considerately
so as not to wake people up
not that I care about it particularly any more
or about the notion of the rejection experience
on the theoretical level. Something is wrong
with a relationship anyway in which a participant
evinces no hostility toward another participant?

There was one thing I remember over and over
Dear love how like you this or rather
how do I like it myself since you won't get a look
Fine but there could be a lot better timing
and the juxtapositions make me edgy so that I
start talking to myself but I'm writing it all down
in dramatic form like several monologues
or role-playing is what it's valuable as probably.

The Prudence Crandall House in Canterbury, Connecticut

The other day when we were driving back from the Yale Game on
   back roads "into blue obscurity,"
we went past the most divine house with the most incredible
   rooflines
and excellent cornices and quoins, in Canterbury.
It's the Prudence Crandall House, and she bought it in 1833 for
   $2000
and nobody knows when it was actually built but it was there in
   1815,
and Miss Crandall started an academy in it which is to say the
   equivalent of a high school
at the behest of the Canterbury residents. Meanwhile, Prudence had
   a black servant
named Sarah Harris whose father was William Lloyd Garrison's
distributor for the *Liberator,* the abolitionist newspaper. Well, Sarah
asked to come to class, and naturally Prudence let her
and that was her big mistake, because the citizens objected,
reasonably as they thought, since they had hired Prudence for their
   white daughters.
So Prudence went off to Boston and had an exhaustive talk with
   said William Lloyd Garrison,
and *he* said she ought to open a boarding school in Canterbury
for black girls, and he gave her the names and addresses
of lots of free black families who could afford it! Aha!
Prudence dismissed her white students and recruited black ones,
telling the enraged townspeople that she was going to teach
   whomever she wanted to.

The citizens, embattled for fair, held a lot of private meetings
and then a Town Meeting, to wheedle Prudence out of it.
Prudence wouldn't budge, and the first black student arrived
on April 1. The citizens got up a petition which resulted in the
   passage

of the so-called Black Law, and black is what it was

because it said that no person could cross the state line into
     Connecticut to be educated there if the people in the town
     where the education was going to take place didn't want them
     to (this idiotic act was fortunately repealed in 1838).

Anyway, back in June of 1833 Prudence was arrested for transgress-
     ing the Black Law,

spending the night in jail, which humiliated the citizens, for some
     reason, but not Prudence.

The newspapers, abolitionist and otherwise, had an absolute field
     day.

Three trials took place, the first with a hung jury, the second with a
     conviction

which was thrown out on a technicality, and the third acquitted her.

The abolitionist press was extremely disappointed when she got off

because they'd hoped to get a lot of mileage

out of appealing the case to the Supreme Court and really making a
     splash.

Well, the acquittal made the Canterbury residents, on the other
     hand, completely beside themselves,

and they threw stones through all of Prudence's beautiful windows
     and put manure down the well,

the students were excommunicated from the Congregational
     Church across the street,

and the doctor wouldn't treat them when they were sick.

But now while all these indignities were going on and on, Prudence
     had gotten married

to a Baptist minister named Calvin Philleo

who convinced her no, it won't do, give up the school. She sold the
     house, they traveled: New York State, Illinois; she taught, they
     settled, gentlemen songsters,

finally in Elk Falls, Kansas, of all places, where she lived till past the
     War and well into Reconstruction. No children.

Fresh Horses Should Be Waiting

The lady and
Julia try to help
with the horses
Fresh horses should be waiting
for the tired riders and there should be oats and
    blankets, Julia,
for the sweating ones they leave; we must
    walk them
up and down and up and down—Oh God,
that's the boring part of horses, not the manure.

An observation
period
Get the men a large kettle of water with dipper
    and ice;
their rugs and robes spread out very well on
    the ground.
Get them tiny brandy glasses with gold fruit
    pictured on them. Get them brandy.
We can lie down along the fringes now that it
    is dark
and stroke the backs of their arms while we listen
    to them sing.

The centuries revisit
them unbidden
Children who sit quietly like us and read
    to you aloud
remind us of our puritan forebears or who we
    would have been then
if we had sat thus by what Stevenson called "the
    cold candle"
and uttered little alphabets, a New England
    primitive in your own home.
It was peculiar that they had to wear hats in the
    house.

They look for the
resolution
Dear Julia, you have always been such a comfort
    to me,
walking unembarrassed on every quadrant of
    the map.

David

David rode sensibly over the asphalt reticulations,
his breath as sweet as apples.

"Back from Topeka in your *baba-au-rhum* boots!
Was it boring? The Dervishes are here."

"Fish is inexpensive for a lot of people.
Chowder smooth and easy and gives a Provençal tone."

"I love a harpsichord David but I love you more.
Wendy looks as though she might faint."

"We have not perspired so much from the heat.
It is rustic here, lovely and lonely as the president of Henri Bendel."

"Meantime you cheerfully proceed stateside to an extreme tower
covered with battens and bring me a Mickey Finn."

So soon as she held his arm, she kept from crying.
Then, freckled and muscled, his arm was—oof—fast round her in
    the dark and they heard
the ghastly syndics reciting the Thirty-Nine Articles.

The Cavendish Club

I was fossicking in the bookstacks not long ago over a semantic and
    epistemological botherment
involving a latent appearance of the petrified dative, and ultimately
    languishing over it,
so I got Angela on the horn, and I said Angela
get me the man from DARE, which is the Dictionary
of American Regional English. And I said CASSIDY?
but all I got was the operator and she was a man
and he was in the middle of arranging to have lunch with Angela.
Cassidy is the Man from DARE in Madison,
Wisconsin, who is remembered as the most recent
editor of Bright's Anglo-Saxon Grammar and Reader,
formulated originally by a favorite henchman and trencherman
of James A. H. Murray, the compiler of the OED,
who nearly died of pneumonia in his spongy workshop
and didn't, alas, live long enough to see publication
in 1908. Well, after Angela and I had screeched at each other
over the airwaves of the intercom, to the delight of everybody,
including Cassidy, whom Angela had finally gotten ahold of
(but then we were cut off), I went off to lunch myself, as a matter
    of fact,
at the Cavendish Club, which is a great deal too expensive to
    belong to,
and was named after the gang of thugs which started the Lone
    Ranger on his lifetime of doing good,
the Cavendish gang. In the front hall there is a sofa
completely upholstered in marabou and extremely tickly.
Anyway I was just putting away some of the curried broccoli bisque
    when I was brought the telephone
and it was Mrs. Farley crying AAAUGH! I'm so *depressed,* so I lunged
    on over there.
Mrs. Farley lives at the moment in a reconverted Richardson
    railroad station

which she has caused to be moved to Irvington-upon-Hudson, so
    the lunging took a bit of time;
also she is exceedingly independent and does not have a maid but
    has her dogs answer the door,
a pair of Brittany spaniels who love visitors and would probably kiss
    any burglar to death.

Such IRONY, said Mrs. Farley, it is precisely about the Cavendish
    Club that I want to talk to you.
The problem is that they want to tear it down and make it into
    locker rooms for the Cathedral,
which is practically my favorite parish, with the exception of the
    one in Jackson Hole
where behind the altar there is just plate glass looking out on the
    Tetons, if that's what they are.
Yet I am aware that you are aware that the Cavendish, while
    masquerading as the stuffy retreat of those slightly to the right of
    McKinley,
actually teaches exconvicts to cook very well, harbors meetings of
    feminists and minority groups and physically and mentally hand-
    icapped people,
and that it likewise lets various indigent artists live there almost for
    free, and everyone thinks they are stockbrokers,
so demolition would be ghastly. I couldn't get the bishop
but I got one of his very sensible auxiliaries, who said that the
    desserts at the Cavendish
are splendid, and maybe we can work something out.

Being of one mind with Mrs. Farley,
I barked some long-distance orders at Angela, and then began to
    make a huge list
of everyone Mrs. Farley and I could think of who had anything to
    do with anything,
and we spent three days pestering them and then six weeks later we
    got terrific results,
which were that the Cathedral would not tear down the Cavendish
    but would secretly use it for tons of their own programs,

and the Cavendish after a sandblasting would go on existing as it
    always had,
except that it had to be renamed the Fiona Birdsey Agape
    Foundation, in honor of the trustee who coughed up most of the
    muscle and wherewithal.

Thither Mrs. Farley and I recently repaired to toast our (partial)
    triumph, and she revealed to me that it had just been revealed
    to her by the Cavendish pastry cook
that he makes his brownies with the regular Betty Crocker family-
    size brownie mix
but for the ⅓ cup of water he substitutes ⅓ of a cup of Jim Beam
and that's why they're so delicious. Munching some agreeably
    betimes,
I contemplated Angela and a spiffy unknown at a window table, to
    whom I raised my chilly glass.

Green Animals

Miss Brayton clipped the boxwood
leaf by leaf herself
although she had
a gardener
for every tree

The boxwood grow
fantastically in the
architected shapes
the gardeners taught them
There every hedge
winds around a green
boxwood animal

llamas made of trees
a green rabbit
a bear with its arm around another bear

Miss Brayton called her house
Green Animals
It looks at Narragansett Bay
The boxwood garden
doesn't mind the salt
It flourished then
It flourishes now

Miss Brayton invited
Hope Slade from Providence
weekend after weekend
year after year

and when Hope was married
and dressing for her wedding

in the morning
Miss Brayton sent
her driver in her car
full of white flowers, full of them
all the way to Providence

so Hope's mother's house
was covered with white
vases and nosegays   bunches
urns of branches and flowerpots   bouquets
buckets of white arms of flowers
and there was no place to sit down

Rachel and Wally

That girl needing rescuing out there in the boat
—her friend is back hysterical on the shore—
the former the girlfriend of that boyfriend of each
of whom it was observed this morning when we saw them hitch
but picked them not up, on the way to our boring aunt's
place up in Portsmouth, New Hampshire: these kids these days!
at their nonsectarian coed day and boar
ding school of rustic suburban rightish stance!
popping with rhetorical questions, afloat
in blancmange literally or swimming in it, says:
the wrong sestet hooked up with the right octave?
Would I swallow that, hook line and sinker? "Not wav
ing but drowning" (Stevie Smith) and yet
remember the dryads are the ones that are never wet.

The House Party

We were invited to a house party last weekend in Lake Forest,
    Illinois, which I shall not soon
forget, and this is not only because I brought what turned out to
    not be the right clothes for it,
but, more objectively, the people were alarming at best.
When I got up in the middle of Friday night there were lots of the
    guests
running through the hall and leaping in and out of each other's
    rooms together,
who mercifully didn't see me. I had to call them all
by their first names, even though I shall never see any of them
    again,
such as Davenport and Davis, Manfred, Ritzinda, Conall, and
    Yvette.
I remarked to Davenport when we were playing croquet that my
    second son at the age of three had cleverly been wont
to refer to croquet mallets as golf hammers, at which Davenport
    laughed not at all;
yet, to be fair, realizing that he had been less than sympathetic, he
    very kindly told me
the plot of the Thorne Smith novel he'd been reading the previous
    night, although I bet that's not all he was doing.
Davenport confided to me over several pousse-cafes that he is a
    grain arbitrator,
and then Manfred came along and they talked about grain.
Usually I like to talk to men, but it was difficult to talk to these,
or difficult for them to talk to me at any rate, but that was OK
because it transpired that the women talked together a great deal in
    little pockets.

Ritzinda true to her name wore a dress that had only one shoulder
and not much of that on Saturday at dinner.
Mrs. Farley told me I should put apricot oil on my face a little at a
time and it would be absolutely wonderful,
much the way Davenport talked about grain, although I certainly
don't think Mrs. Farley was in the apricot oil business.
Ritzinda of the single shoulder asked me who I'd gotten to get me
invited,
and looked somewhat addled when I said that a cousin of a college
classmate of Yvette's had been my brother's piano teacher
and that some of these shared the same dentist in Georgetown,
which is all perfectly true, if boring. Mrs. Farley
may possibly be a hundred and goes around completely covered
with Liberty scarves,
and as one might expect there was dancing Saturday night well into
Sunday
at which she excelled, scarves and all, and it turned out she had
known the violinist as a young man.
Some of the other things we talked about were Carl Rogers,
shallots, bargello,
tobacco barns, curare, giving people *la question* during the French
Revolution and after,
encaustics of the tobacco barns, which are Yvette's idea of *lares et
penates,*
David Riesman, James Agee, and exchange students in the
Philippines.
Mason, to whom I am married and whose job is teaching church
law to seminarians for a living and with whom I went to this
house party,
and who incidentally got the better of the deal, can't figure out why
I'm being so disagreeable,
inasmuch as *he* spent the whole weekend in the study with a
marvelous and very complete collection of church law books

dating back incredibly far in their original bindings, and reading
    practically all of them,
and showing up for meals and cocktails during which he explained
    to Emery and Rosfrith Van de Sand
the complete history of church law, which if they had been going to
    seminary would have cost them
thousands and thousands of dollars, and they didn't even have to
    buy the texts,
although the Van de Sands probably couldn't have gotten admitted
    to seminary anyway
even if they'd wanted to; but of that they will doubtless remain
    forever unaware.

Sol Invictus

"Christ the true sun is risen in the dying of the day,"
something those anonymous Christian aborigines knew perfectly
    well
in the winter solstice, mixing up Easter with Christmas.

Various folk plays, waits and mummings persuade us
likewise of the virtue of portents, and the Bayeux Tapestry people,
Romanesque fellows—ISTI MIRANT STELLA—they marvel at the
    star

which in fact is a comet, with their egg-like eyes.
But the song that went along with it all is sung and gone,
being oral-formulaic and sidereally "lost,"

unlettered; and then there's the problem of liturgy
vs. literature, because where does one leave off
and the other begin? and what about Baumstark's

Second Law, which says that the most important
parts of the ritual remain in their original languages?
Oh, the holy day is connected to the stones of cities

(where were *your* spiritual ancestors at the problematic parting of
    the *soi-disant* Red Sea?
arguing about pig bones in the wilderness of Lachish?
or painting themselves blue and worshiping fir trees?)

and to a monomythic talisman such as the relic,
except you can't *have* a relic if there's a resurrection,
and you certainly can't have a horn from the ox

at Bethlehem, since the ox was a late fabrication
from an apocryphal gospel factory. Nor a tailfeather

of the Holy Ghost. The point is that the physical object
is thought to impart sacramental energy, a touchstone
in the material suffused with the divine, composed
of not so much Christmas or Easter, orgy and trauma,

as a safe and solemn passage to other places—here's where
the monomyth comes in again—the bearer
is a shapeshifter in a curious chariot whose days are lengthening!

About Calder

In my own view, friction fittings are small monuments
even though you say they aren't practical like a threading
I love them and I love cogs too on bikes
Whoever invented them I'd like to shake his hand

A painter stays at our house—he is painting our children
and in the morning it takes him ages to make himself scrambled
    eggs
whipping and folding them as if they were colors
But then finally he is saying: Zee sobway ees feeneeesh!

I am writing to you about Calder
his metallurgy   his space minerals
Once when it was way below zero my hand stuck to one of the discs
—risky, inductive, and prime, and also scattered, I remember

CAROLINE KNOX's previous books are *The House Party,*
To Newfoundland (The University of Georgia Press, 1984 and 1989),
and *Sleepers Wake* (Timken, 1994). Her poems have appeared in
American Scholar, American Voice, Harvard, Massachusetts Review,
New Republic, Paris Review, Ploughshares, Poetry, and elsewhere.
She has received awards from the National Endowment for the Arts,
the Ingram Merrill Foundation, the Yale/Mellon Visiting Faculty
Program, the Massachusetts Cultural Council, The Fund for Poetry,
the Senior Fellowship Program of the Fine Arts Work Center in
Provincetown, and *Poetry* magazine (the Bess Hokin Prize).

THIS BOOK has been set in 10/14 Adobe Caslon. William Caslon released his first typefaces in 1722. Caslon's types were based on seventeenth-century Dutch old style designs, which were then used extensively in England. Because of their incredible practicality Caslon's designs met with instant success. Caslon's types became popular throughout Europe and the American colonies; in fact, the printer Benjamin Franklin used Caslon almost exclusively. The first printings of the American Declaration of Independence and the Constitution were set in Caslon. For her Caslon revival, designer Carol Twombly studied specimen pages printed by William Caslon between 1734 and 1770. The roman is considered a "workhorse" typeface due to its pleasant, open appearance, while the italic is exceedingly decorative.